CREATING A
LOCAL HISTORY
ARCHIVE AT
YOUR PUBLIC LIBRARY

D1738763

ALA GUIDES FOR THE BUSY LIBRARIAN

CREATING A LOCAL HISTORY ARCHIVE AT YOUR PUBLIC LIBRARY

FAYE PHILLIPS

AN IMPRINT OF THE
AMERICAN LIBRARY ASSOCIATION
CHICAGO   2017

FAYE PHILLIPS is the owner of V F Phillips Consulting specializing in library and archival services, local history research and publications, and appraisal. From 1986 to 2012 she was a librarian, archivist, administrator, and associate dean at the Louisiana State University Libraries in Baton Rouge. Her publications include works on local history, and the administration of archives and special collections. She has designed and taught courses on local history, archival practices, preservation and digital libraries.

ALA Editions purchases fund advocacy, awareness, and accreditation programs for library professionals worldwide.

Extensive effort has gone into ensuring the reliability of the information in this book; however, the publisher makes no warranty, express or implied, with respect to the material contained herein.

ISBN: 978-0-8389-1566-0 (paper)

Library of Congress Cataloging-in-Publication Data

Names: Phillips, Faye, author.

Title: Creating a local history archive at your public library / Faye Phillips.

Description: Chicago : ALA Editions, an imprint of the American Library Association, 2017. | Series: ALA guides for the busy librarian | Includes bibliographical references and index.

Identifiers: LCCN 2017009979 | ISBN 9780838915660 (pbk. : alk. paper)

Subjects: LCSH: Libraries--United States--Special collections--Local history materials.

Classification: LCC Z688.L8 P485 2017 | DDC 026--dc23 LC record available at https://lccn .loc.gov/2017009979

Cover design by Kim Thornton.
Text composition in the Charis SIL and Soho Gothic typefaces by Alejandra Diaz.

♾This paper meets the requirements of ANSI/NISO Z39.48–1992 (Permanence of Paper).

Printed in the United States of America
21   20   19   18   17   5   4   3   2   1

CONTENTS

ACKNOWLEDGMENTS

OF ALL THOSE who assisted in the completion of this book, I particularly thank:

- Jamie Santoro, ALA Editions editor, who is efficient, helpful, and patient; and
- Kathy Marquis, Public Services Librarian, Albany County (Wyoming) Public Library, for encouraging me to present a proposal for this book to ALA Editions;
- Florence Jumonville, Louisiana and Special Collections Librarian Emerita, University of New Orleans, for editing and content advice;
- Melissa Eastin, Baton Rouge Room, East Baton Rouge Parish (Louisiana) Library, who manages an exemplary local history archive; as well as
- Nicole Davis, Photography and Media Archivist, and Grace McEvoy, Archives Media Specialist, Austin History Center, Austin (Texas) Public Library;
- Rikki M. Chesley, Head of Archives & Special Collections, Athens-Clarke County (Georgia) Library;
- Derek Gray, Special Collections Archivist, DC Public Library, Washington; and
- Machteld Schoep, PR/Photographer, Mecanoo architecten, Oude Deltf, the Netherlands, for photographs of the Martin Luther King, Jr. Memorial Library, Washington, DC.

INTRODUCTION

IN *LOCAL HISTORY* *Collections: A Manual for Librarians,* Enid Thompson defined the materials of local history and gave simple advice for handling them.[1] Thompson's manual, a 1978 product of the American Association for State and Local History, was a successful and useful guide for professionals and nonprofessionals involved with the care of local history archives. In 1995, I wrote in *Local History Collections in Libraries* that the addition of personal computers and national databases to the library world, the development of national standards for the arrangement and description of archives and manuscripts, the acknowledgment that collecting policies and documentation strategies were needed, and advances in preservation technology all called for a new look at local history archives in libraries. By that time, more technical data than Thompson provided about the arrangement and description of archives and manuscripts was needed. Advances in national databases through regional networks and through OCLC and the Library of Congress meant that, for the first time, manuscript and archival records were entered into national databases along with books. Today in 2017, yet another new look at local history archives is relevant and timely.[2]

Creating a Local History Archive at Your Public Library is a comprehensive manual and a guide. For archivists, the value of this manual is one of continuing practical education and theoretical development. The value to librarians is essentially the same, but the book also provides guidelines for the administration of non-traditional library materials. In 1995, the World Wide Web was amazing, dazzling, frightening, and new to most archivists and librarians. The possibilities of its value to our work and purpose were embraced and, at the same time, ridiculed as science fiction, often by the same professionals as well as the public. Now, the convergence of the Internet with local history archives in public libraries aids researchers and the public, gives new tools to librarians and archivists, and points to continued improvements in saving and sharing local history in public libraries.

In their recent book, *Local History Reference Collections for Public Libraries*, Kathy Marquis and Leslie Waggener wished for a manual to aid in the tasks of assembling and managing the most helpful local history collections possible in public libraries. One part of such a collection is the category of reference materials (Marquis's and Waggener's focus). Another part includes archives and manuscript materials. My desired task is to add a potential manual for the later to their manual on the former.

In collaboration with ALA Editions, Marquis and Waggener surveyed librarians for their book. Almost 90 percent of the 649 responders answered yes, their library had a separate local history section. Of these collections, 63 percent contained unpublished manuscript or archival materials, 69 percent held photographs, and 76 percent held a variety of ephemeral materials. Many of those who wrote fuller comments on the survey requested more extensive information on providing access to and caretaking of these archival collections. A few commenters asked for help in starting a local history archive.

The Society of American Archivists Public Library Archives/Special Collections Roundtable conducted a survey of its nearly 960 members in February 2013. Of the 82 members who responded to the question "In which kind of repository do you work?" a majority (52.44 percent) indicated that they work at a public library. Their job titles varied, but 40 listed "archivist" and 31 listed "librarian" as their main job titles. In response to the question, does your work specialize in a particular area, most respondents (51 of 78) stated they specialized in local history, while 37.18 percent specialized in rare books and manuscripts, and 14.10 percent listed records management. Eighty-three percent stated that they joined the Society of American Archivists Public Library Archives/Special Collections Roundtable (PLASC) to learn more about archives and special collections in public libraries. When asked what services they would like PLASC to offer, 66.67 percent of 75 respondents wanted more continuing education opportunities. Others wanted the Roundtable to present discussions on how to start an archives or special collections library, and how archivists and librarians can assist teachers in their classrooms. The things they valued most about the Roundtable were networking opportunities, learning and information-sharing opportunities, and support from and identification of like-minded librarians and institutions.[3]

Marquis and Waggener's research and the SAA Survey confirm a need for concise, practical guidelines to best practices for the acquisition, access, and care of archival and manuscript formats within public library local history collections. *Creating a Local History Archive at Your Public Library* hopefully meets this need. Training for archivists sometimes includes minimal public library practices, and librarians' training seldom includes archival course work. Bridging these gaps in knowledge for professionals responsible for the local history archive is one goal of my guidebook. The book will help librarians and archivists build a knowledge base from which to better utilize archival and library theory and to advance their continuing education.

Much has been said in the last decade about *hidden collections*—those that are not accessible because of a lack of cataloging and processing. Local history archives in public libraries, whether begun today or a hundred years ago, always seem burdened with backlogs of materials awaiting attention. Librarians and archivists work to protect and make accessible inherited collections, even as they acquire more collections in the twenty-first century. This book will provide archivists and librarians responsible for local history archives in public libraries an understanding of how to better manage, make accessible, and preserve their collections. Issues relating to legacy collections are discussed as well as those related to starting a local history archive. Included in this book are practical, current, and cost-effective solutions with step-by-step guidelines and examples from many of today's most successful public library local history archives. Chapters show progressive steps for planning, processing, and providing access to collections. If, however, the local history archive's current need is for processing advice only, that chapter can serve as a standalone guidebook. Another goal of this book is to explain each element of managing a local history archive, illustrate why each element is important, and present steps to complete each element. What is it? Why is it necessary? And, how do you do it?

Eric Linderman, in his 2009 article "Archives in Public Libraries," said, "There is no available manual for developing an archives program specifically for public libraries."[4] My purpose is to present a manual to help fill this need. The primary users of this manual are public libraries' local history archives staff, such as curators of manuscripts, archivists, subject librarians, special collections reference librarians, and manuscripts processors, as well as paraprofessional staff. Others who will find the book helpful include administrators, division directors, reference librarians, catalogers, history subject specialists, genealogy librarians, and public history librarians. Any library with a local history archive will find helpful guidance here.

Futurist Roger E. Levien in "Confronting the Future: Strategic Visions for the 21st Century Public Library," places local history collections at the center of possible future scenarios for public libraries. He projects that, as the library moves from the physical to the virtual and eventually from a role of a portal to the role of an archive, and as the library serves as a place of creation not just collection, its "enduring storehouse" of knowledge will be based on local history materials. This storehouse will be created and cataloged by the library that has assumed the responsibilities for "capturing and maintaining the unique materials that record local life." Local history archives in public libraries are critical to the future.[5]

Local History Collections in Libraries in 1995 listed only printed resources in the bibliography—no online sources and no websites. In 2017, *Creating a Local History Archive at Your Public Library* includes numerous citations for online articles and website resources, as well as printed articles and books. From 2012 to 2017, five substantive publications with guidance relevant to developing and administrating a local history archive in the public library were issued in print.[6] I'm delighted that the canon of resources for the management of local history archives has grown to help us all now and in the future. Let the dialogue continue.

NOTES

1. Enid Thompson, *Local History Collections: A Manual for Librarians* (Nashville, TN: American Association for State and Local History, 1978).
2. Faye Phillips, *Local History Collections in Libraries* (Englewood, CO: Libraries Unlimited, 1995), 1.
3. Kathy Marquis and Leslie Waggener, *Local History Reference Collections for Public Libraries* (Chicago: ALA Editions, 2015); Society of American Archivists Public Library Archives/Special Collections Roundtable (PLASC), 2012. www2.archivists .org/groups/public-library-archivesspecial-collections.
4. Eric Linderman, "Archives in Public Libraries." *Public Libraries* 48 (January/February 2009): 48.
5. Roger E. Levien, "Confronting the Future: Strategic Visions for the 21st Century Public Library," *OITP Policy Brief 4* (June 2011): 25, ALA Office for Information Technology Policy, Publications.
6. Jeannette A. Bastian, Megan Sniffin-Marinoff, and Donna Webber, *Archives in Libraries: What Librarians and Archivists Need to Know to Work Together* (Chicago: Society of American Archivists, 2015); David W. Carmicheal, *Organizing Archival Records: A Practical Method of Arrangement and Description for Small Archives*, 3rd ed. (Walnut Creek, CA: AltaMira Press, 2012); Pam Hackbart-Dean and Elizabeth Slomba, *How to Manage Processing in Archives and Special Collections* (Chicago: Society of American Archivists, 2012); Marquis and Waggener, *Local History Reference Collections for Public Libraries* (Chicago: ALA Editions); Carol Smallwood and Elaine Williams, eds. *Preserving Local Writers, Genealogy, Photographs, Newspapers, and Related Materials* (Lanham, MD: Scarecrow Press, 2012); and Gregory S. Hunter, *Developing and Managing Practical Archives*, 3rd ed. (New York: Neal-Schuman Publishers, 2017).

CHAPTER 1 | # DEFINING, CREATING, AND DEVELOPING A LOCAL HISTORY ARCHIVE

> Local history is, of course, the most accessible of all history, for it is closest to home.
>
> **–Carol Kammen, On Doing Local History**

THE HISTORY OF LOCAL HISTORY

Local history archives are focused on the people and culture of an area over time for the benefit of current and future citizens. Free public libraries provide extensive local history services to their communities and have done so since the mid-nineteenth century. New Hampshire passed the first legislation authorizing the use of public taxes in cities and towns to maintain free libraries. Massachusetts followed in 1851. On March 20, 1854, the Boston Public Library, known as the first free municipal library in the United States, opened its reading room in a temporary space. Works on local and family history have been collected and made available since the library began. Local history materials about Boston are prevalent, but Massachusetts and most of New England are covered as well. The New York Public Library has collected local history materials since 1910 in its Division of U.S. History, Local History &

Genealogy. Local history archives in public libraries are often part of special collections, and, as such, may or may not be housed in facilities separate from the main library. Public libraries with small staffs and collections sometimes administer local history collections as an extension of the reference or public services departments.

The study of local history and the collecting of local history materials in the United States had its first flowering in the 1820s and 1830s, when numerous states founded historical societies. By 1900, there were 2,000 historical societies throughout the states and territories. Social libraries, however, such as Benjamin Franklin's Library Company of Philadelphia began providing book collections for paid members in the colonial era. Gifts in the 1750s of histories of the American colonies, including Pennsylvania, could perhaps be considered the first local history books in this forerunner of the public library. In 1762, an actual circulating library— lending two books, including novels, per circulation for a fee—opened in Annapolis, Maryland. In the 1830s, free black men and women established social libraries in New York and Philadelphia. By the end of the nineteenth century, private and society fee-based libraries evolved into free public libraries supported by public taxes. From 1886 to 1917, philanthropist Andrew Carnegie gave funds to build libraries in 1,412 communities that committed to provide building locations and to support operations of the library with local taxes. Citizens viewed the public library as a trusted entity where their personal collections of local history would be saved. The second great wave of interest in the development of regionally focused collections and the writing of professional local history grew from the celebration of the US Centennial in 1876. At that time, the stated missions of many historical societies were to publish histories and to gather and preserve documents and materials of their local area.

Also in 1876, the US Bureau of Education issued *Public Libraries in the United States of America, Their History, Condition, and Management: Special Report* and presented it at the Office of Education's exhibit at the Centennial Exhibition. According to the report, free public libraries (like free public schools) were established and maintained on the same principles. Libraries fulfilled "for all a function similar to that which the college libraries perform for those fortunate enough to pursue a college course; rightly administered they are indeed what one writer has called them, 'the people's colleges.' , , , The free public library is equally generous to those who have and to those who lack. It cares as tenderly for the many as for the few." A central part of the first public libraries' missions was the preservation of history and culture.[1]

Local history collections focus on local history, and local history focuses on a certain geographic location and the past of that location. Essentially, it is history from the perspective of a community, state, or region. Carol Kammen, one of the most widely known local history teachers and leaders, explains that local history, "which seems to be the simplest, the most straightforward of disciplines, is actually a most complicated arena of activity," because multiple strands of activity must be combined. Local history reflects upon what happened in a particular place—what was written, recorded, and preserved. It can also be a broad field of historical study, even though it has a limited geographical focus. Local historians could be any and all of us, whether we refer to ourselves as creators, writers, researchers, collectors, preservationists, archivists, librarians, photographers, educators, conservators, catalogers, or some combination—anyone who spends their time in some way focusing on the history of a place.[2] It might be easier to identify what is not local history and who is not involved, as all history contains a bit of local history.

During the 1960s, the social history and public history movements spurred a new emphasis on local history. Many libraries developed new collecting programs for local and family history materials, and courses on these subjects were added to college curricula. Historians, perhaps as a reaction to changes in society, predicted that an exploration of local history would broaden the concept of national history. Throughout the 1960s and 1970s, public libraries directed programs for minority groups of citizens and established resource centers to collect materials on ethnic history.[3] History teachers on all levels included regional, state, and local history in their classes.

A local program that began in Cleveland, Ohio, in 1974 eventually grew into the National History Day competition for grades 6–12 (https://www.nhd .org). Students participate in school, regional, and state academic contests to determine those that will compete in the National History Day contest. Its mission is "to provide students with opportunities to learn historical content and develop research, thinking, and communication skills through the study of history and to provide educators with resources and training to enhance classroom teaching." Also in the 1970s, the National Park Service revised exhibits to reflect changing historical trends with focus on industrial sites and the lives of African American women from humble origins. In 2012, the National Park Service stated that it continues to "implement new interpretive programs designed to broaden perception of the common past."[4]

The 1976 US Bicentennial celebration had an even greater impact on public interest in developing local history archives in public libraries. The Bicentennial lit the fires of genealogical research and took it to a new level. In 1977, Alex Haley's genealogical novel *Roots* and its conversion into a television miniseries further ignited the public's interest in local history. Genealogy and family history researchers discovered archival collections and demanded that their public libraries collect, preserve, and provide access to original documents to aid their research. In 1996, one of the first and most successful online databases for genealogical research began, and by 2009, it combined with several other databases under the title and website of Ancestry.com. Academic historians followed trends and again included community and family history in their research and in their classroom lectures. Since the 1990s, subcategories of history were widened to include cultural, ethic, family, local, oral, urban, public, women's history, and many other subjects that developed out of the new social history of the 1960s. Other facets of local history came in 1966 with the passage of the National Historic Preservation Act. In 2016 (the fiftieth anniversary of the act), researchers were looking again at the local history of the built environment preservation movement.[5]

Today, the history of minority and ethnic groups in certain geographic locations—small communities, both rural and urban, along with the social changes within those communities—and the history of people who left few written records are notable fields for the local history archive. Social history areas long ignored conventionally are still significant, because they focus on ordinary people and their activities, institutions, and culture. Upper-class people created less history than we formerly believed, and the majority—the unknowns—created more that reveals just as much about the past (and about change) as do studies of the elite. Archivists, librarians, and historians are compelled to collect and write local history that includes all people and all historical aspects—essentially remaking maps of the past by leaving nothing out. All can use the local history archive to learn about the history of their groups, and the collections' primary sources provide broader avenues for student learning. Through documenting the activities of local citizens and organizations, a historical record of the archives' users and those who will use it in the future is maintained. Local history resources help build factual, balanced understandings of what happened, how it happened, and perhaps even why it happened.[6]

SCOPE AND FORMATS OF MATERIALS

Users of the local history archive, whether social historians, economic historians, or genealogists, seek information in many types of materials. Manuscripts document the lives of individuals, families, and other self-identified groups, while archives document the lives of organizations, institutions, businesses, and governments. Both further the quality and quantity of information about the local area. A key to meeting the needs of users is to collect all varieties of materials relating to the local area and integrate them through proper cataloging.

Manuscript collection types and formats include diaries, account books, financial records, memoirs, journals, logs, scrapbooks, typescripts, videotapes, compact discs, digital files, photographs, and correspondence to or from individuals. Some manuscripts are the papers/records created by an individual or family. Then there are the manuscripts that were collected by someone other than the creator. For example, a collection titled "The Jack Johnston Collection of Mark Twain" indicates that Johnston collected manuscript material of and about Mark Twain. Johnston did not create the Mark Twain material, but because he brought the items together, the collection bears his name.

Archives can consist of the same types and formats of materials, but they are the records created by an organization, business, institution, or government, as opposed to those created by individuals, families, or other groups. The archives of a university, business, church, or non-profit organization can contain financial records, committee files, personnel records, public relations materials, correspondence, minutes of meetings, policies and procedures, organizational charts, directories, audiovisual materials, web files, machine-readable/electronic records, and even newspaper morgues. Local history departments within public libraries are often designated as the official archival repository of the city and county governments but might also include archival records produced by the League of Women Voters, the Rotary Club,

FIGURE 1.1

Librarian Mary Ternes works at a Lektriever file sortage machine used to store and access the *Washington Star* photograph and clippings collections, pre-1972.

Courtesy DC Public Library, Washingtoniana Division.

local churches, and garden clubs, as well as the business records of banks, florists, lumber mills, and clothing stores.

Archives and manuscripts are valuable because they correspond to the information contained in published materials and serve as the basis for primary research. Economics, social life, personal viewpoints, religion, and politics are only a few of the topics found in manuscripts. A diary kept by an early pioneer to the area might dispel or confirm local legends. Letters from a local soldier serving in Vietnam can show the effect war had on the individual, the family, and the community. Photographs taken over several decades depict the growth or decline of an area. Hand-drawn maps of battle sites and river crossings expand users' knowledge of local events.

Other formats in the local history archive include measured drawings, audiovisual items, oral histories, machine-readable records, and artifacts. Measured drawings are a source of information about buildings in the local area. Architects, engineering firms, building contractors, and interior designers keep records of their work and plans of buildings. A historical file of measured drawings aids in understanding the growth and development of a community, as well as its economic and social changes, and is valuable for historical preservation and remodeling of buildings.

Audiovisual materials are also important. Photographs, slides, videocassettes, reel-to-reel and cassette tape recordings, phonograph records, and films discuss local people, places, and institutions and how they change. The earliest examples of photography—daguerreotypes and ambrotypes—can be found in personal manuscripts and in the records of photographers' businesses. The value of photographs cannot be overstated. They can corroborate or disprove both written and verbal sources. Illustrations for publications and promotional materials for businesses can come from the photograph collection. Excellent books on identifying, collecting, and preserving historic photographs are available.[7]

Television news broadcasts, films of college and high school athletic events, professional movies made in the area, promotional films made by the Chamber of Commerce, sound and video recordings of city council hearings, and family videotapes of local events (such as parades) are invaluable sources of history and culture.

Audio formats are also valuable. Recordings of speeches by local personalities, reminiscences of town elders, and music performed by local artists are aural reminders of local history.

Oral history can be expressed by the verbal rendition of folk tales, eyewitness accounts of historical events, or interviews about the life of an individual. A volunteer can do interviews by using appropriate questions based on research. Such interviews, once transcribed and made available, fill gaps in the written record. Oral history is an avenue for completing the historical record of institutions where key decision-making is done verbally (such as the US Senate). Through oral history, scholars can gain knowledge about the action of governing boards, city councils and state legislatures. Videotaped oral history interviews create both an aural and a visual record.

Not all materials for the local history archive are available in their original form. Writers, school boards, businesses, hospitals, churches, architects, and local governments use personal computers, laptops, and tablets to compose, and then store their files in the Internet "cloud." Libraries and archives use computers similarly. The original draft of a Pulitzer Prize-winning novel by the area's most famous author might exist only on a computer disk. The writer's donation can include manuscripts of plays, novels, and poems, printed copies of such items, and the computer disks on which the drafts were written. Because of computers, architects no longer need preliminary paper sketches of their original ideas for a building. Organizations and institutions create organizational records through desktop computers, intranets, and the Internet, which are stored in house and in the cloud. Machine-readable digital records are difficult for even the most sophisticated and well-financed repositories to manage, especially since technology changes rapidly.

Electronic records of institutions, social organizations, and businesses might include word-processed correspondence, reports, annual reports, memorandums, personnel files, and any other type of document normally found as paper records. Such documents can be printed and kept as paper files, if necessary. Other digital records might include those with data that are most useful in their original computer format, such as spreadsheets, surveys, opinion polls, and marketing statistics. A printout of these files loses the context of the data, along with manipulability. Included in donations will be records that are born digital, as well as paper and photographical materials scanned into digital files. Personal papers and family papers will include similar documents and files that are machine-readable—some originally digital and some scanned into digital files. The data might arrive on a variety of media, including CD-ROMs, internal and external computer hard drives, USB drives, and access to cloud/Internet drives.

The local history archive might contain three-dimensional objects, including swords, dolls, toys, china, silverware, and jewelry. Artifacts such as these belong more properly in the local or state museum, but transfers are not always possible when no museum exists or if the state museum cannot accept more materials. In some instances, if the local history archive is to maintain good donor and community relations, it is best to accept and keep artifacts. Artifacts can be used to enhance displays in the library and can be loaned to others for exhibition through cooperative agreements. When artifacts are kept, they should be identified, cataloged, and made accessible to researchers.

Artifacts are not the only unusual items found in archives. Items such as bumper stickers, political buttons and broadsides, playbills, flyers, art works, underground newspapers and pamphlets, religious manuals, and cookbooks might be donated to the library. Staff must make decisions, based on the department's collection development policy, whether or not certain artifacts will be accepted for the archive.

Aspects to consider before starting a local history archive are increased collecting (versus timely access), space, staff capabilities, budgets, planning, public relations, preservation, and security. Finally, the question of how the local history archive will be built into the structure of the organization must be answered. Public library staff would be responsible for starting a local history archive, updating the guidelines and procedures for an existing archive, resurrecting a long forgotten archive, and/or a bit of each.

MISSION STATEMENTS

Before beginning or revitalizing a local history archive, write a mission statement and obtain administrative approval of it. Public libraries "support a common collective mission: providing access to information, knowledge, and resources."[8] Mission statements for a local history archive emphasize this and its role in acquiring, preserving, and making accessible to the community materials about the local area. The mission statement succinctly explains the department's purpose, defines its vision, and explains its place within the larger institution—the public library—while detailing and more narrowly defining the department's philosophies apart from the public library's broad mission. What other divisions or units of the public library have mission statements, and how is the local history archive mission statement tailored to the others? Without such synergy, it will be difficult for the public library administration to adopt the department's mission statement. Approval at the highest level establishes the authority of the department to exist and carry out its work.

Mission statements for all levels of the public library should answer these three questions: who, what, and how. Who are the users of the collection, what services do they receive, and how are the collection materials acquired and made accessible? As its name implies, a local history archive is targeted to users who expect preserved and accessible collections of primary source materials.

Also, a thorough reference collection is needed. Some local history reference materials will be most helpful if housed in the department. Kathy Marquis and Leslie Waggener have provided an excellent model in their book,

Local History Reference Collections for Public Libraries. The broader public the department hopes to serve probably will include researchers from beyond the local area who also expect access to these materials. Today's users are local and non-local, in-person and online—and so will be future users. Local history materials that are available for present and future generations to explore at the library cannot be fully replicated online. Research can be supplemented by online access and digital reproductions, but hands-on interaction with original archives and manuscripts cannot be replaced. Mission statements reflect these concerns. However, be aware that, because of their importance to the success of the library and its departments, mission statements are difficult to prepare and approve.[9]

Local history archives will fit seamlessly into the overall public library mission if its mission answers who is served, what does the local history archive do, and how are goals accomplished. For example, it could be said that the local history archives serve local communities, outside researchers, genealogists, and historians. The department would meet these service needs through collecting and preserving resources and "developing awareness of local history and making these materials available."

One archivist suggests this example as a mission statement: The purpose of the local history archives is "to preserve the materials that document the history and heritage of [name of geographical area] and to provide access to the community, to the general public, and to researchers." Others suggest that the mission statement include some policies, such as "items do not

FIGURE 1.2

Austin History Center reading room in 2012.

Courtesy of the Austin History Center, Austin Public Library. Photograph by Grace McEvoy.

circulate." The statement could also include procedures, such as how the materials will be made more widely known within the community through marketing activities.[10]

■ Mission Statement Examples

The Austin Public Library Vision Statement (library.austintexas.gov): Austin (Texas) Public Library is key to making Austin a dynamic creative center and the most livable city in the country. Austin Public Library Commitment: The Austin Public Library is committed to providing easy access to books and information for all ages, through responsive profession-als, engaging programs and state-of-the-art technology in a safe and friendly environment.

The Austin History Center's mission is to procure, preserve, present and provide the historical records that make up Austin's unique story. As the local history division of the Austin Public Library, the Austin History Center provides the public with information about the history, current events, and activities of Austin and Travis County. We collect and preserve information about local governments, businesses, residents, institutions, and neighborhoods so that generations to come will have access to our history.

Ontario City Library Mission Statement (www.ontarioca.gov/library): We strengthen our community by creating and supporting lifelong reading, learning, and enjoyment. Vision: The Ontario City (California) Library is your place to connect to each other and the world—where you are inspired by our materials, innovative programs and services, and are delighted by our commitment to the community.

The Robert E. Ellingwood Model Colony History Room of the Ontario Public Library was established in the Ontario City Library in 1970. The room contains non-circulating materi-als concerning the social, economic and governmental history of Ontario and the western region of San Bernardino County.

East Baton Rouge Parish Library Mission Statement (www.ebrpl.com): The East Baton Rouge Parish (Louisiana) Library is a community service organization that connects our citizens with information, resources, materials, technology, and experiences in order to make a positive difference in their lives.

The mission of the Baton Rouge Room of the East Baton Rouge Parish Library is to collect, manage, preserve and provide access to items that represent current and historical actions of local governments, businesses, residents and institutions of the City of Baton Rouge and East Baton Rouge Parish. These items include but are not limited to photographs, manu-scripts, documents, periodical publications, audio and video recordings and memorabilia.

MANAGING

Every local history archive, whether large or small, requires appropriate administration. The manager relies on policies and procedures, a staff, a budget, and a plan, in order to properly administer the department. In spite of the endless amount of literature written about management, the principles are simple, straightforward, and largely a matter of common sense. Management includes planning and setting policies and procedures. A local history archive in the public library needs policies for collection development, copyright, access, preservation, security, and disaster preparedness.

Policies and Procedures

Having made the decision to collect, preserve, and provide access to local history collections, a road map is needed. Policies are the road map, and procedures are the road signs. Policies deal with each level of the parent library's organization and, while some policies are unique to the local history archive, most policies affect all levels and departments of the library. Procedures, or actions, are subordinate to policies. Procedures implement policies—they are the way for, and methods of, directing the most efficient and productive work.

Policy is a verbal, written, or implied boundary to the general direction for managerial action. Policies come from outside and inside the organization and can be imposed, implied, or originated. Imposed policies that come from outside the organization include state and federal laws such as copyright and minimum wage that are essential to formulating in-house policy and are therefore inflexible until laws change. Policies that come from inside the organization are those created by the organization itself. Implied policies are those that people assume are policies because of what goes on around them. For example, the administrator of an organization might receive first choice in the vacation schedule. While this is only tradition and not a stated policy, staff members might assume that it *is* policy because it has always been done that way. Originated policies guide the general operations of the library and flow from the objectives reached through planning. Polices for the local history archive, therefore, give the staff guidance in operating the collection. At what point should a staff member seek assistance from the department head about a difficult patron? What is the department policy on photocopying or photographing copyrighted material? Under what circumstances may patrons view original items restricted because of physical condition? The answers to such questions form policies.

Procedures translate policies into actions and behaviors. For example, a procedure might outline how a user may or may not read or handle archived items that are restricted because of condition. It might specifically state that a group of visitors may not physically interact with restricted items without prior arrangements and a designated appointment time. It might further stipulate that even frequent users must make an appointment to review restricted materials. Both situations require the presence of a local history archive staff member at all times.

Policies and procedures can also relate to personnel issues. Policy sets how much time an employee receives for annual vacation, and procedures implement that policy. Procedures detail how staff members can request vacation time, how that time is scheduled, and how records of leave are maintained.

All local history archives need the following policies:

- Collection development policy (discussed in Chapter 2).
- Access policy (discussed in Chapter 3).
- Copyright policy (discussed in Chapters 2 and 3).
- Preservation, security, and disaster policies (discussed in Chapter 4).

Policies and procedures are essential to maintain consistency and provide the department with adequate administration. They are necessary for each function, including acquiring, processing, referencing, and cataloging materials. An up-to-date manual containing an administration's policies and procedures for each function of the local history archive eliminates the need to make decisions on the same questions, over and over. Once managers resolve a question, they document the decision and make it a policy. The policy and procedure manual is a communication tool for all staff members. All manuals should be made available through the parent library's intranet, wiki and/or other internal communication sites.

But how do policies and procedures come to exist? They follow from long-term and short-term planning.

Planning

The saying that "in this world, nothing can be said to be certain, except death and taxes" is attributed to Benjamin Franklin. If Franklin had lived in the late twentieth and early twenty-first centuries, he could have added *change* as another certainty. Financial challenges, technology, users' needs, and laws, among many other things, create change for libraries. Change factors in the twenty-first century make planning imperative. The University of California

San Diego Library found that in 2008–2009, "economic challenge and digital opportunity met head on, leaving the libraries a perfect storm as the backdrop for strategic planning." While this book's purpose is not to teach strategic planning, it does present a background on strategic planning, gives reasons why planning is important, and suggests how local history archive staff can be and should be involved.[11]

Libraries can face challenges and find opportunities through planning by beginning with strategic plans for the future. The act of thinking strategically helps the library continue to move forward while handling challenges. Strategic, long-term plans derived from mission and vision statements are coupled with yearly follow-up, short-term plans. Some factors affecting planning are external: budget problems, the economy, technology, patterns of use, and users' satisfaction and dissatisfaction. Other factors are internal: staffing patterns, employees' increased technological knowledge, staff expectations, library space limitation, and the economy, to name a few.

One particular internal concern is resistance to planning by library staff and leaders due to fear of the changes implied by planning. Strategic planning is relevant for libraries. But in reality, other than the performance of yearly budget preparations, few examples of current strategic planning—and the hoped-for subsequent yearly planning—can be found. Although planning is implied by the policy and budget preparations recommended in the excellent "RUSA Guidelines for Establishing Local History Collections," a section about planning is not included. (Visit www.ala.org/rusa/resources/guidelines/guidelinesestablishing for more information.)

Strategic, Long-Term Planning

The responsibility for formulating a library's strategic plan belongs to the administrative team, but all staff members are responsible for carrying it out. Successful strategic planning involves the staff on every level gathering the opinions of stakeholders (users, governing boards, and government leaders) and understanding the forces, both internal (space and budgets) and external (laws), that affect the environment in which the library exists. Local history archive staff members can expect to be called upon to lead portions of the strategic planning activities, serve on various planning committees, gather feedback, and write or edit documents related to the strategic plan. All library departments—including the local history archive—have value to add to the planning. Proactive involvement pays dividends for the department. Each department's functions, needs, and holdings must be reflected in the goals and objectives of the strategic plan.

■ Definitions*

Strategic information management (SAA, 373): The skills that enable professionals and organizations to make well-informed decisions that result in a competitive advantage in the business world. Strategic information draws on principles of records and information management, information technology, and strategic management.

Strategic planning (ODLIS): The systematic process by which a company, organization, or institution (or one of its units) formulates achievable policy objectives for future growth and development over a period of years, based on its mission and goals and on a realistic assessment of the resources, human and material, available to implement the plan.

*Many of the definitions throughout this book are from the Society of American Archivists, Richard Pearce-Moses, *A Glossary of Archival and Records Terminology* available online at www.archivists.org/glossary; and Joan M. Reitz, *Online Dictionary for Library and Information Science (ODLIS)* available online at www.abc-clio.com/ODLIS/odlis_s.aspx.

In her book, *Starting an Archives*, Elizabeth Yakel lists four steps to successful planning:

1. Identify and articulate a broad goal, either long-term or constant each day.
2. Formulate as many flexible objectives as needed to reach the goal.
3. Devise realistic activities (also known as action items) to accomplish objectives.
4. Establish who is responsible for each activity and what materials are required to complete the activity, and the date when the activity is to be completed.

Bruce W. Dearstyne explains this fourth step with style in *Managing Historical Records Programs*: "Programs need to develop and follow plans in order to ensure steadiness of purpose, make optimal use of resources, signal to employees, executives, and customers alike what the program intends to do, focus the work, and take the program in new directions as needs, challenges, and opportunities change." Implicit within Dearstyne's planning purpose statement is the acceptance by a local history archive and its parent agency of the hard work and commitment required for success.[12]

All policies—and the procedures to carry out the policies—require planning. A local history archive within a public library will be governed by the planning activities of the library's administration. Local history archive managers and staff will benefit themselves, the department, their patrons, and their future by becoming knowledgeable about library management, administration, and planning. Staffing and budgeting for the department are part of the long-term and short-term management plans of the parent library, with each department having its own regular line of funding in the library budget. The local history archive requires a mission-based planning document that includes long- and short-term goals developed according to the requirements of the library administration. Formulated goals in planning must resolve the overlap of users needs and the capabilities within the physical and financial constrains of the library to provide services. Goals are action oriented, and objectives specify how to achieve the goals; both goals and objectives must be flexible, timely, and changeable. Librarians and archivists need to ask what is realistic and what is obtainable. Long-range, broad plans are those that reflect the expected status of programs three to ten years ahead. In the long-range plan of the library, a goal to increase grant funding by 25 percent over a five-year period requires the local history archive to increase the amount it raises during that period.

■ Strategic Plan Example

Library's strategic plan Goal 1: Each year from 2017 to 2020 increase use of the library's resources by 10 percent.

Local History Archive Goal 1

Goal: Outreach–increase use of the Local History Archive.

Objective: By December 20, increase the awareness and use of local history resources by a specific user group (high school seniors) by 10 percent.

Activities:
1. After gaining permission from high school administrators, outreach and reference staff will send invitations to 12th grade social studies teachers to attend an introductory session.
2. Reference, access, and acquisition staff will prepare presentations for the introductory sessions and suggest proposed projects aligned with accepted lesson plans.
3. Outreach staff will follow-up by scheduling class visits for students.
4. Reference, access, and acquisition staff will work with students' assigned projects in the local history archive.
5. All staff will evaluate the outcomes (student project grades, willingness of teachers to bring future classes, and anonymous student comments).

Resources needed:
1. Handouts
2. Information page on library's website
3. Staff time

■ Examples of Public Libraries' Strategic Plans Online ────────

In 2015, the Gwinnett County (Georgia) Public Library announced a new strategic plan in the *Georgia Library Quarterly*. The plan for 2015–2018 includes new mission and vision statements, and focuses on three main goals: 1) increase awareness of the library and its services, 2) pursue outreach and engagement, and 3) address community needs. These goals are designed to provide guidance for the development of library programs and services over the next three years. The plan represents the community's vision for the library while navigating the technological, societal, and demographic challenges of the future (www.gwinnettpl.org). The library and community also began discussing the implementation process for the strategic plan.*

"Discover Unlimited Possibilities @ Your Library" is the East Baton Rouge Parish Library's strategic plan for 2014–2019. The brief executive summary states that the Library seeks to serve "all residents as an educational, informational, recreational, and cultural center through a wide variety of resources, services, and programs." The East Baton Rouge Parish Library, according to survey and interview results, has been successful in its efforts and has satisfied users and loyal supporters. Within the strategic plan are ways to expand upon the library's success by concentrating its efforts in customer experience, technology, programming and collections, facility improvements, employee development, and marketing and outreach to the community. The entire strategic plan and a summary are available on the website at www.ebrpl.com.

*"Gwinnett County Public Library, GCPL Announces Strategic Plan," *Georgia Library Quarterly*, 52 (Art. 15, 2015). The plan is accessible under the "About" link and presented in a PDF format through Google drive (www.gwinnettpl.org).

───

Levien's "Confronting the Future: Strategic Visions for the 21st Century Public Library," (www.ala.org/offices/sites/ala.org.offices/files/content/oitp/publications/policybriefs/confronting_the_futu.pdf) intends to "assist in the development of effective strategies for American public libraries by delineating the elements of alternative visions for libraries in the coming decades. It does not recommend particular visions; rather, it suggests a process libraries can follow to make their own strategic choices based on their specific situations." Through strategic visions, libraries can convert the challenges into opportunities that will make greater contributions to the individuals and communities they serve. Even though manifestations of some of these future visions are already being seen in libraries, the visions are not for the near term (within the next few years) but for the longer term (over the next few decades). To meet the changes and challenges of the future, libraries must make strategic choices in four distinct dimensions where changes will most often confront them:

1. Facilities and media (physical, virtual, or both).
2. Individual or community focus.
3. The library (a physical or virtual collection library, or a creation library).
4. The future portal library, which is completely virtual, or an archive library that holds unique local materials, both physically and virtually.

Each dimension consists of a continuum of choices lying between two extremes. These dimensions are currently occurring and are likely to continue to occur in the future. No strategy, even one based on careful and dedicated thought, can be considered immutable.

The Forsyth County (Georgia) Public Library (www.forsyth.public.lib .ga.us) strategic plans for the years 2013–2018 were developed utilizing Levien's strategic visioning. The Forsyth County Public Library report presents and explains "four 'continuums,' each continuum located between two 'strategic vision' extremes." The visions are not beginning and ending points; instead, the reader considers where her library is on each continuum, and where she wants it to be. For example, the goal of a library is not necessarily to move from a totally physical library to a totally virtual library, but rather to determine what percentage of physical and virtual materials and services it wants. On the second continuum, a library decides if its future focus will be on individual users or on making the library a community-gathering place. The same process is used for continuum three: Is the library a place that acquires materials or a place where materials are created? For continuum four: Is the library a hub (portal) to other resources throughout the world, or is it a repository (archive) of all available information in all formats on a selected subject field such as local history? The continuums are not mutually exclusive; a library can be a totally physical archive, a totally virtual archive, or both.[13]

■ Example Strategic Choice Dimensions

Current	Midpoint	Future
Where the library should be at the end of the current strategic plan period		

Totally Physical (facilities and media)	◀ Today	Future ▶	Totally Virtual (facilities and media)
Individual Focus	◀ Today	Future ▶	Community Focus
Collection Library (physical or virtual)	◀ Today	Future ▶	Creation Library
Portal	◀ Today	Future ▶	Archive

There are, of course, crosscutting themes among the dimensions, including librarian competencies, collaboration and consolidation, digitization, personal and social networking, archiving and cataloging, and pricing.

Levien's emphasis on local history archives in his strategic visions for the future is striking. He sees a future in which archives—rather than purely virtual/portal libraries—take on more and more responsibility for the collecting and archiving of locally relevant collections. Librarians will play the lead role in establishing "the data organization, the metadata vocabulary and structure, and the means of tracking of provenance." While many of these materials will be accessible via the Internet, non-digital media and local librarians' knowledge about the materials require a physical library to provide for users' needs. "At the other extreme of the portal/archive dimension lies the local public library that serves as the enduring storehouse of local knowledge and information" (as many do already). The library will assume responsibility for local materials that will be digitized to the extent possible and linked to the Web or its successor. Librarians "will have to face issues of data preservation and transfer due to the aging and obsolescence of digital media of all forms. Taken together, the network of thousands of public libraries, each performing this function locally, would establish an unmatched data resource to answer a multitude of possible questions by accessing data from one or many of these locally based archives." The library's website will host meetings and groups whose interests would be the subjects and formats of the community materials, whether contemporary or historical.[14] An example of such a service is the Digital Amherst website of the Jones Library in Amherst, MA (www.digitalamherst.org).

Many public libraries provide a wide range of services aimed at adults, ranging from film shows to invited speakers who are often local authors. Libraries increasingly offer programs and develop exhibits that respond to local needs and interests. These offerings draw people into the library while serving an important cultural and social function. Although other venues, such as historical societies, art galleries, and museums, also perform this function, libraries can focus their efforts on subjects that meet specific needs of their patrons and are not covered by other agencies. The public library performs one function for which there is no alternative: It is a unique symbol of the extent of a community's commitment to saving informational, educational, and cultural values.

Budgeting

The local history archive in the public library requires a published mission statement—a statement of its purpose, for without a clear mission, the chances for a department to develop and function effectively are limited. Effective development requires adequate financial resources. Administrative adoption of the mission statement presupposes budget support and a mandate for the local history archive to carry out its specified programs. Budgets include funding for ongoing staffing, facilities, future maintenance and preservation issues, equipment and supplies, acquisitions, description and access of collections, outreach and special projects, and continuing education for staff members. The department head must carefully maintain financial and budget expenditure records to present analyses to the administration on the costs of the department's functions. The budget and its preparation are plans tied closely with all other long- and short-term plans, and it is critical to include the local history archive as part of the library's planning process.[15]

Before embarking on revitalizing a local history archive or establishing a new one, prepare a potential budget as an operational, short-term plan, at three levels: minimal, acceptable, and ideal. The minimal budget sets out costs to: 1) reinvigorate an old local history archive or create a new one, 2) maintain the collection and make it accessible, and 3) secure and staff it. A minimal budget probably will not allow for digital projects, extensive outreach, or an active collecting program, but it will allow the archive to remain operational. An acceptable budget lists costs necessary to: 1) collect, maintain, and make accessible collections, 2) do outreach, 3) plan digital projects, and 4) staff and secure the collection. An ideal budget will cover all the costs in an acceptable budget but to a higher level and with funds to begin digital projects, instead of just planning to have them in the future. Not even an ideal budget will be the Rolls Royce level of funding, but if accepted and funded, it means your local history archive will continue from year to year. The local history archive requires the appropriate commitment from all levels of the administration and a continuing budget allocation.[16]

Every librarian and archivist needs to know the basics of accurate budgeting. The first rule is to understand where the money comes from and how it is allocated. The parent library might use one type of budget or a combination of several types, but regardless of which type of budget is used, the local history archive manager must understand it and the ramifications of its use in order to be as effective as possible. Many librarians and archivists receive only a brief introduction to budgeting in university courses. However, continuing education courses in management, budgeting, and planning can assist those who are managers and those who aspire to be managers.

As an example, the local history archive's short-range plan within a given year is to improve the quality of research collections by preserving and cataloging a noted photography collection. To achieve this goal, staff members are assigned the activity of applying for outside grant funding to preserve and catalog the collection. They work with library administrators, the conservation department, processing archivists, financial officers, and other appropriate staff and departments to develop a grant proposal. If grant funding is received, an objective for the following year will be to carry out the grant project in the local history archive.

Planning benefits everyone in the library and the community. This is hard to see when staff members are overworked, underpaid, and the backlog of uncataloged materials and uncollected acquisitions grows each day. However, planning creates an opportunity to review the daily activities of the local history archive and consider why they exist and why they do or do not work. Careful, well-produced plans can create a local history archive that defies budget cuts and broadens its appeal to the community. Plan to plan.

Staffing

The department might include several groups of workers: a combination of full-time and part-time professionals and paraprofessionals, students, volunteers, and grant-funded employees. Staff allocations and money to pay personnel come from the library administration, which can also determine what type of staff the department receives. Grants received can provide extra— although time-limited—staff positions. In most public libraries, candidates with a master's degree in library and information science from a school accredited by the American Library Association are hired for professional librarian positions. Professional archivist positions in public libraries also require an accredited library degree with an archival component as part of the training. Frequently, archival certification through the Society of American Archivists is also required. Each public library system, as part of a city or county government, follows the position requirements for professional and paraprofessional positions as established by the local government; thus, the public library probably has little flexibility regarding required credentials of potential employees. Hopefully, the local history archive will have flexibility in preparing position description job functions to fit its unique staffing needs.[17]

Current personnel theory maintains that all tasks must be measurable in some manner. For example, a reference archivist might be required to answer 90 percent of all reference questions accurately. The manuscript-processing archivist might be required to produce finding aides to three collections each quarter. The objective, of course, is accountability. How well does the person perform the assigned tasks? The problem inherent in such a system is going so far to the extreme that professional responsibilities are demeaned to the quantifiable. When this happens, quality in performance suffers, sometimes even when quantity does not. Job descriptions written fairly, accurately, and comprehensively help. A vague description of a task such as "works at the local history archive reference desk" is not acceptable. To answer appropriate reference questions thoroughly and accurately in person, by phone, or by letter/email, is a precise task description. Job descriptions also assist in yearly performance evaluations of staff.

As with employment procedures, public libraries' administration of staff is overseen by the local government's personnel departments. This includes performance evaluation procedures, the timing of evaluations, and reporting. Supervisors can, however, apply thoroughness, candor, sensitivity, and timeliness to discussions. If supervisors and employees review performance on a regular basis, then annual, formal performance evaluations become painless. Ignoring poor quality work is unacceptable, and counseling is effective only when done frequently, not just once each year. Employees who perform poorly deserve an opportunity to improve performance through accurate evaluation at the earliest time after a problem is observed. It is the supervisor's responsibility to ensure that employees are aware of their ratings at all times. Each employee should be given monthly or even weekly opportunities to discuss job performance with the supervisor.

Collecting for the local history archive will be guided by appropriate collection development policies, along with the procedures and objectives needed to implement and carry out such policies. Chapter 2 discusses collection development policies and the procedures layered within them.

SCENARIOS

These scenarios describe two possible local history archive departments in public libraries. Questions and examples throughout the following chapters refer back to these scenarios.

Scenario A

The Everytown Public Library Local History Archive

The Everytown Public Library opened its first building in 1876. Inspired by the US Centennial, the librarians encouraged gifts of local history items from the community. The community rewarded the library with printed materials, a complete run of the town newspaper, genealogical charts and family histories, church bulletins, and advertising ephemera from local businesses. The Rivers family donated a scrapbook, photographs, and sermons written by Rev.

Tom Rivers in the 1860s. Rivers & Sons deposited some 1860s business ledgers from its founding company, Rivers Railroad Supplies. John Jones loaned family papers related to his ancestors, the first African American family to establish a cattle range in the county, and records of their business, the Jones Saddle Company. A small room with numerous windows was designated the Everytown History Room.

The Rivers family migrated to Everywhere County in the late eighteenth century, and the Jones family arrived in the 1840s. Descendants of both families still reside in the same area in the twenty-first century. The biographies of individuals in the family show that the Joneses were cattle ranchers, saddle makers, small-business owners, musicians, educators, community leaders, abolitionists, and politicians, among other things. Members of the Rivers family were ranchers, farmers, small-business owners, ministers, writers, military men and women, politicians, and a number of other things including community leaders and social misfits. The Rivers and Jones family histories are closely tied to Everytown and Everywhere County's history.

Over the following century, citizens gave to and deposited with the library a variety of printed and non-printed materials related to local history, including several hundred photographs. The photographs all depicted town and county history as well as state history, but were received from almost 100 different people and date from 1864 to 1995.

Everytown and Everywhere County were prosperous and growing, except during a few periods of their history. Prosperity fostered three branch libraries and a new main library building. The first building was designated as one of the branch libraries, and the Everytown History Room remained in that building. In 1995, the community agreed that a new main library building with modern capabilities was needed. Sondra Rivers volunteered to lead the building fundraising campaign and to serve as the community representative to the Everytown Public Library's new building planning committee. During her work with the library, Sondra discovered the Everytown History Room, which contained manuscripts and records of her ancestors.

Despite a lack of space, the librarians had added local history materials and developed a genealogy collection in all the library's branches in response to community requests before and after the US Bicentennial. More recently, an online subscription to Ancestry.com was purchased and, along with many other electronic resources, was available to the community through the library's website 24 hours a day. Spurred on by Sondra Rivers' discovery of her family papers and records in the Everytown History Room, a number of people brought new donations and deposits of local history archives and manuscripts. In response, Jane Doe was designated the Local History Librarian. Jane had spent as much of her time as possible since she began working at the library in 1992 on acquiring and processing local history print materials. She also assisted people who wanted to use the local history non-print materials, had created local subject vertical files for ephemera and photographs, and indexed some of the archives and manuscript collections. In 1998, with a small grant from the Everytown Historical Preservation Foundation, Jane purchased archival folders and boxes for many fragile documents and window shades to block out some of the sunlight in the Everywhere History Room. Also in the history room, Jane found files of the Everywhere County Board of Education, 1900–1932; the Women's Christian Temperance Union scrapbooks; and a handwritten history of the Vietnamese colony in town. Luckily, Jane was a member of the new library building planning committee and made the recommendation that a new Everytown History Room be included in the plans.

The new Everytown Public Library main branch building with a proper space for archives opened in 2009. Jane hired an assistant who was trained as an archivist. The new archivist's first task was to determine the title, provenance, condition, and ownership of the non-print collections. The second task was to plan on how to proceed with the goal of making the collections accessible to the public.

Scenario B

Neighbor Village Public Library Local History Archive

The Neighbor Village Public Library opened its first building in 1905. Inspired by the Centennial of Lewis and Clark's expedition and that year's World's Fair, the librarians encouraged gifts of local history items from the community. For a few years, the community responded by donating or depositing genealogy files, some scrapbooks, a few photographs from the Neighbor Village Baptist Church, a large box of undated and unidentified newspaper clippings, a notebook with recipes pasted in it, scattered issues of the town's newspapers, and items from the Smith family and the Bacon family. A corner of the Reference Room near the newspaper reading room was designated as the Local History Collection.

The Smith family migrated to Neighbor County in the late eighteenth century, and the Bacon family arrived in the 1840s. Descendants of both families still reside in the same area in the twenty-first century. The biographies of individuals in the family show that the Smiths were cattle ranchers, saddle makers, small-business owners, musicians, educators, abolitionists, and politicians, among other things. The Bacons were ranchers, farmers, small-business owners, ministers, writers, military men and women, politicians, and a number of other things, including community leaders and social misfits. The Smith and Bacon family histories are closely tied to the histories of both Neighbor Village and Neighbor County.

Gifts and deposits of local history items slowly stopped arriving, and the library's small staff had no time to actively seek other materials for the local history archive. As the library building became more and more crowded, the local history corner space was reallocated to the reference section. Non-print items in the local history collection were put into the windowless storeroom for duplicate materials, exchanges, and supplies. After World War II, the library building, including the storeroom, was updated with central heat and air conditioning.

In 1960, Neighbor County entered a very prosperous era, and the community supported a new library building. When the new library building opened in 1966, the first building was designated a branch library. Also in 1966, Jack Smith's favorite grandmother died. Virginia Smith was a prominent member of the community, a leader in many local business organizations, a local politician, and a genealogist. Jack Smith wanted to write and publish a biography of his grandmother, so he began his research by reading newspaper microfilm at the new library building. Jack soon realized that he wanted to do more by writing a history of the entire Smith family and their role in the histories of Neighbor Village and Neighbor County. He needed to gather the archives and manuscripts of the Smith family from 1782 to the present. Jack asked the advice of his good friend, librarian James Dotson. James Dotson had worked at the public library for five years and, while helping sort and identify materials to be moved to the new library building, discovered in a storeroom the materials formerly collected for the Neighbor Village local history archive. James knew Jack would want to see the box in the storeroom that was labeled "Smith Family."

James, however, wanted to be sure of the ownership of the Smith Family box of materials first, before talking to Jack. James had taken some continuing education courses in local history and archives over his career, and he knew provenance and ownership information as well as finding aids were needed for all the non-print materials he found labeled "Neighbor Village Local History Archive." How did James proceed with the goal of making the collections accessible to the public? How did the Neighbor Village Public Library begin again on the right path to establishing the Neighbor Village Local History Archive?

NOTES

1. United States, Office of Education, *Public libraries in the US of America; their history, condition, and management. Special report, Department of the Interior, Bureau of Education, Part I* (Washington: Government Printing Office, 1876), xiv, 401.
2. Carol Kammen and Norma Prendergast, eds. *Encyclopedia of Local History*, 2nd ed. (Lanham, MD: AltaMira Press, 2013), 296; Carol Kammen, *On Doing Local History* (Walnut Creek, CA: AltaMira Press, 2003), 4.
3. Page Smith, *As a City Upon a Hill: The Town in American History, Vol. 2* (New York: Alfred A. Knopf, 1966), vii; Wayne A. Wiegand, *Part of Our Lives: A People's History of the American Public Library* (New York: Oxford University Press, 2015), 199–200.
4. Denise D. Meringola, *Museums, Monuments, and National Parks* (Amherst: University of Massachusetts Press, 2012), 167.
5. David L. Ness, book review, *Indiana Magazine of History* 75 (1996): 369–371; See the website "Preservation 50, Commemorating 50 Years of the National Historic Preservation Act," www.preservation50.org.
6. Terry Walker, "Local Treasures: The Value of Special Collections in the Public Library Setting," Washington Library Association, *Alki* (July 2014): 21; Linderman, "Archives in Public Libraries," *Public Libraries* 48 (January/February 2009): 47.
7. Mary Lynn Ritzenthaler, Diane Vogt-O'Connor, Helena Zinkham, Brett Carnell, and Kit Peterson, *Photographs: Archival Care and Management* (Chicago: Society of American Archivists, 2006); Robert Hirsch, *Seizing the Light: A History of Photography* (Boston: McGraw-Hill, 2000); and Alan Trachtenberg, *Reading American Photographs: Images as History, Mathew Brady to Walker Evans* (New York: Hill and Wang, 1989).
8. Gwen Glazer, "Digitizing Hidden Collections in Public Libraries," *OITP Perspectives* 1 (June 2011) ALA Office for Information Technology Policy, 1.
9. Barbara B. Moran, Robert D. Stueart and Claudia J. Morner, *Library and Information Center Management*, 8th ed. (Santa Barbara, CA: Libraries Unlimited, 2013), 78; Walker, "Local Treasures," 18, 21; and Richard J. Cox, *Managing Institutional Archives: Foundational Principles and Practices* (Westport, CT: Greenwood Press, 1992), 27.
10. Bastian, Sniffin-Marinoff and Webber, *Archives in Libraries*, 13, 16–17; and William Helling, "Creating Local History Collection Development Guidelines," in Smallwood and Williams, *Preserving Local Writers*, 106, 113.
11. Jeff Williams, Tammy Nickelson Dearie, and Brian E. C. Schottlaender, "Bottom-Up Strategic Planning: The UC San Diego Libraries Experience," *Library Leadership & Management* 27 (213): 2; Masanori Koizumi, "Transitions in Public Library Management: From the International Perspective of Strategy, Organizational Structure, and Operations," *Journal of Library Administration* 54 (November 2014): 660.
12. Elizabeth Yakel, *Starting an Archives*, (Chicago: Society of American Archivists, 1994), 20, 22–23; Bruce W. Dearstyne, *Managing Historical Records Programs: A Guide for Historical Agencies* (Walnut Creek, CA: AltaMira Press, 2000), 49.
13. Carla Beasley, "Forsyth County Public Library Strategic Planning, 2013–2018." *Georgia Library Quarterly*, 50, 2 (Art. 9, 2013), 17. The article is an example that applies Levien's theories. Unfortunately, the strategic plan does not appear on the website www.forsythpl.org as published in the *GLQ*. See http://digitalcommons .kennesaw.edu/glq/v0150/iss2/1.
14. Levien, "Confronting the Future," 26.
15. Cox, *Managing Institutional Archives*, 32–33; Linderman, "Archives in Public Libraries," 48.
16. Moran, Stueart, and Morner, *Library and Information Center Management*, 409–414; Bastian, Sniffin-Marinoff and Webber, *Archives in Libraries*, 79, 84.
17. Phillips, *Local History Collections*, 121–127; Dearstyne, *Managing Historical Records Programs*, 50–57; Bastian, Sniffin-Marinoff and Webber, *Archives in Libraries*, 39–40, 82–84.

CHAPTER 2 | COLLECTION DEVELOPMENT POLICIES FOR THE LOCAL HISTORY ARCHIVE

> As community anchor institutions, public libraries must provide an avenue to locally specific materials that cannot be found elsewhere. In essence, they must keep local history alive and connect it with its greater context.
>
> **–Gwen Glazer, "Digitizing Hidden Collections in Public Libraries,"** *OITP Perspectives*

DEFINING AND BUILDING a new local history archive (or reinvigorating a dormant one) in the public library challenges even the most skillful librarians and archivists. Reviewing the scope of materials previously collected, as well as planning for future collecting in a new or old department, however, is an exciting aspect of the job. Collection development policies and procedures, donor relations, planning, and acquisitions through gifts and sometimes purchases are integral parts of building a local history archive.

Every public library has its own mission centered on the desire to collect and make available materials for their patrons. To carry out its role in the mission of the parent institution, each local history archive requires an individual collection development policy that derives from and coordinates with the library's policy. If possible, the policy should be modeled on collection development policies previously adopted for other units. However, the local history archive will differ from other units because of the formats collected such as archives and manuscripts.

Planning begins with a written collection development policy. An early (1976) but still relevant guideline from the American Library Association states that a written collection development policy is a tool to assist in consistently working toward defined goals, to ensure stronger collections and wiser use of resources. More recently, in 2012, the ALA Reference and User Services Association issued "Guidelines for Establishing Local History Collections," in which the first point under the collection development section suggests to "write an acquisitions policy for collecting local history materials." At the end of 2016, the Society of American Archivists, Acquisitions & Appraisal Section, Best Practices Subcommittee conducted a survey to gather information about current policies for acquisitions and collection development. The survey is part of SAA's on-going project to provide examples of existing policies and create resources for policy writing. Survey results will be published on the SAA Acquisitions & Appraisal Section "Assigning Value" Blog www .appraisalsaa.wordpress.com.[1]

Written policies inform users, employees, administrators, government officials, colleagues, and the public of the nature and scope of the collection, as well as the plans for its development. Libraries try to identify their users' requirements and establish priorities for fulfilling them through policy statements that are regularly reviewed so needed changes in collection areas can be indicated. Although libraries and archives can grow without a collection development policy, most need policies to plan, develop, and evaluate the collection as budgets and space continue to change. Policies work best when they precede active collecting rather than being developed as an afterthought. Sporadic, unplanned, competitive, and overlapping collecting has in the past led to the growth of local history archives of marginal value. Library administration, the community, donors, and users see collecting policies as signs of the program's maturity and accountability, as evidence that the local history archive is a growing, reliable research resource, and as proof that the program is proceeding responsibly.[2]

As discussed in Chapter 1, written planning documents are outlines of the steps to be taken to reach future goals and are today's designs for tomorrow's actions. Effective policies are 1) reflective of the objectives and plans of the organization, 2) consistent, 3) flexible, so that they can be changed as new needs arise, 4) distinct from rules and procedures (policies allow for latitude, but rules and procedures remain firm), and 5) written. Librarians/archivists know that the management of change through policies is a complicated but positive course of action rather than reaction and holds the department steady while facing change. A written collection development policy prevents archivists from becoming involved in unplanned activities, the acquisition of unwanted materials, and inflexibility in program planning. The expected use of the materials, and the users as well as the donors, can impact the local history archive's developmental focus.[3]

The collection development policy will be reevaluated and changed as needed to meet goals. A thoughtfully constructed and maintained collection development policy includes: the archive's scope of physical and intellectual content (such as African-American history and women's history), format restrictions (Can the library preserve computer files from the 1970s and a variety of sound and video formats?), and instructions for deaccessioning. Embedded within the collection development policy are a gift policy, a cooperative-agreement policy, and a resource-sharing policy. A model collection development policy contains the following basic elements:

- Mission statement
- Priorities and limitations
  - Users/patrons served
- Types of programs supported
- Gift policy
- Deaccessioning policy
  - Resource sharing/collaboration/cooperation policy
- Procedures affecting the policy and its implementation
- Procedures for monitoring development and reviewing the evaluations[4]

For an example, see the East Baton Rouge Parish Library, Baton Rouge Room Policies and Procedures, Special Collections Collection Development Policy (http://ebrpl.libguides.com/BatonRougeRoom).

As discussed in Chapter 1, after a mission statement is written and adopted by the library administration, other parts of the collection development policy can be completed. The purpose of the organization is defined in the statement of purpose or mission statement, and is periodically reviewed and analyzed. The local history archive's statement of purpose agrees with and flows from that of the parent library, and assists in fulfilling the mission of the public library system.

EXAMPLE MISSION STATEMENTS | See Chapter 1, page 10.

PRIORITIES AND LIMITATIONS OF THE LOCAL HISTORY ARCHIVE

Priorities and limitations of the local history archive are also detailed in the collection development policy. What are the present strengths? How do these strengths meet the needs of the programs and the users served? Specify which fields—history, literature, culture, or folklore, for example—are represented most voluminously or qualitatively in the collection. What is the level of research to be served, and how does that research affect the archive's policies? The research level is tied closely to institutional affiliation and initial materials acquired. Staff assigned collection development responsibilities seek to develop collections that meet the research needs and requirements of users. Few can become exhaustive research centers collecting everything published, as well as unpublished manuscripts and records, about the local area. Therefore, the research level is defined as it applies to each organization.

Is the department's purpose to acquire all archival and manuscript materials about a particular member of the community or a particular school or organization? Or, is it to preserve a representative sample of all fields and subjects for a particular time or event (for example, the pre-Civil War history of the town or only folklore archives and manuscripts relating to the community)? Is it focused on a specific time period, or does it include materials from all periods? Are all subject areas relevant to the local area collected, or are there limitations (such as not collecting church records)? What subjects are marginally represented, and will the collecting of archival and manuscript materials for these subjects continue at the present level, expand to fulfill the local history archive's mission and the needs of its users, or cease because the subject is no longer part of the collecting policy? What are the present identified weaknesses (such as gaps in World War II history coverage to show how severely the large ratio of local men killed in battle impacted the local community)? What materials on this subject will be collected?

Specify the geographic limit of the local history archive: town, county, state, or region. It might focus only on local genealogical information and not the history of businesses in the area. In which languages other than English are materials acquired, and why? Are materials in Portuguese accepted because there is a significant Brazilian immigrant population in the area or because Portuguese peoples settled the area? What forms or formats will be included—microforms, audiovisual items, printed materials, computer records, manuscripts, web files, and others? Will artifacts and artwork be excluded? Exclusions should also be a part of the policy. For example, a local history archive might seek everything about the area except local church records, because there is a religious archive in the next town. Will Catholic

Church records be excluded because the local diocese has an established archives department providing access to users?

This information helps the librarian/archivist to focus collecting activities and avoid acquisitions of inappropriate materials.

■ Examples, Priorities, and Limitations of the Local History Archive

The Archives @ Queens Library, Long Island Division, New York, combines much of this information in its Mission Statement and in its Collecting Policy (www.queenslibrary.org under the research tab).

Mission Statement: The Archives, housed in the Central Library, exists to preserve, organize, and manage the use of materials which deal with the geography and the natural, cultural, social, economic and political history, both past and present, of the four counties of Long Island. Printed monographs, serials, pamphlets and broadsides, manuscripts, photographs, prints, drawings, map and plans are collected to the comprehensive level. The collection is under the responsibility of the division librarian.

Collecting Policy: The Archives divides its acquisitions into three areas:

- The Archives acquires primary and secondary resources documenting the natural, social, economic, and political history of Queens County in all formats.
- The Archives acquires secondary resources including reference works, monographs, journals, indexes and abstracts, and other published works that document Kings, Nassau, and Suffolk Counties.
- The Archives acquires the records of the Queens Library's Department heads, as well as the organization's publications, board meeting minutes, and other historically valuable records.

The Archives accepts donations and purchases of material that fit within the scope of its collection.

The Grand Rapids Public Library (Michigan) Collection Development Policy under the "Selection of Materials" section contains "Collections with Additional Consideration: Grand Rapids History and Special Collections" with details about what materials are considered (www.grpl.org under the research tab).

The archival collections are composed of original materials of a documentary nature centered on the Greater Grand Rapids area. This might include, but is not restricted to, individual and organizational records, diaries, church records, maps, visual images of various formats, oral histories, scrapbooks, and newspapers from Grand Rapids and its surrounding area.

The library generally does not collect three-dimensional objects or materials that are considered to be realia. Realia and objects are passed on to other institutions with the expertise to collect and house such materials. The archives do not collect the official records of the City of Grand Rapids. Such records are kept with the City Archives and Records Center.

USERS/PATRONS

The collection development policy also defines the users served by the local history archive. Are expected users scholars, freelance writers, graduate students, undergraduates, and/or others? The general public are, of course, expected users and could include students at all levels, local historians, and genealogists. For the public library, the local community within which the library resides contains the primary users, but are there any restrictions? Will younger students require adult accompaniment to the local history archive? Will group projects by students be accommodated? Will the size of the groups be limited? Will non-community researchers be accommodated, especially in a local history archive with limited resources? Will appointments for research times be required? Budgets, number of staff, and space available for reference services will affect the number and types of users the department can adequately serve.

■ Examples Users/Patrons ────────────────────

The Norfolk (Virginia) Public Library Local History and Genealogy Collection states who users are in an inclusive way: "The purpose of the collection is to provide resource materials for individuals conducting local history or genealogical research in the Sargeant Memorial Collection" (www.norfolkpubliclibrary.org).

Others, such as the East Baton Rouge Public Library's Baton Rouge Room, are more specific:

Targeted Users: The unique primary source material of the Baton Rouge Room Collection is made available to all citizens of the City of Baton Rouge and East Baton Rouge Parish Louisiana. This includes the citizens of Baker, Zachary, and the surrounding unincorporated areas. Users of the collection include those interested in genealogy or historical research. Other users include library and parish government staff, students and educators, businesspersons, historic preservationists, journalists, and all other interested persons (see www.ebrpl.libguides.com under the Infoguides tab).

PROGRAMS

Through collection development policies managers define and evaluate the types of programs supported by the collection. Successful programs of the local history archive are geared to the users. These can include exhibits—in house and on the website—that are articulated in the collection development policy. Will the physical exhibits include just in-house exhibits, or will there also be a program to create traveling exhibits? Patrons and donors will want to know whether exhibits will be available as an aid to research and as a product of their donations, and that their gifts will not be exhibited if they so specify. Exhibits of donated materials might require permission depending on copyright. An exhibition program helps facilitate interest in and use of the local history archive, because exhibits serve as an advertisement for the collection, attract researchers and donors, and inform the public about the department's work. In addition to exhibits, other outreach programs to the community include classes, lectures, tours, workshops, blogs, websites, publications, and social media activities for users and donors.

Websites, blogs, digital collections, and even some social media contributions can constitute publication. Before the Internet existed, publications were printed-paper newsletters, bulletins, pamphlets, brochures, magazines, photographs, books, and articles researched within the local history archive. Today, websites present information about ongoing programs that include social media activities and links to social media sites. Both printed and web publications aid research, donor relations, fundraising, and access. Grants, as well as digitization and microfilming projects, can be part of program activities. As seen from these examples, programs can and do overlap. Publications and podcasts naturally flow from blogs, lecture series, and exhibits. Seeking grant funds from various agencies and developing fund raising campaigns for special projects could become programs. Grant funds can pay for preservation of fragile materials, on-line exhibits, or creating access to collections. Inform users and donors about special projects such as these, and seek their involvement.

Inclusion of these elements in collecting policies serves to inform the public, the administration, and the staff of planned activities and programs of the local history archive while providing for flexibility in planning. It also enables the staff to avoid becoming involved in unplanned activities. Once program needs are identified, acquisitions can become more focused.

◾ Program Examples

August 28, 2013, marked the 50th anniversary of the civil rights March on Washington, DC, and Dr. Martin Luther King Jr.'s "I Have a Dream" speech. The Washingtoniana Division of the Martin Luther King Jr. Memorial Public Library in DC commemorated the events with an Oral History Research Center project. Interviewees shared their stories at a public commemorations event. In addition to the oral history project the Division's DC Community Archives collected memorabilia from DC residents who attended the March (see "Special Collections" under the research tab at www.dclibrary.org).

Another program of the Martin Luther King Jr. Memorial Library is the Memory Lab, where patrons have access to equipment to scan, digitize, and save family photographs.

Local history photographs are posted on the Boston Public Library's Flickr Photo Sharing pages (www.flickr.com/photos/boston_public_library).

FIGURE 2.1

In addition to Reference Services, the reading room can provide photocopy machines and showcase exhibits, Washingtoniana Division, Martin Luther King Jr. Memorial Public Library.

Courtesy of Mecanoo architecten, Oude Delft, the Netherlands. Photograph by Machteld Schoep.

GIFT POLICY

The collection development policy defines what materials will be accepted as gifts (as stated in the Archives @ Queens Library policy). How are gifts managed? Potential donors can be given copies of the collection development policy, which lists the types of materials accepted, the subject areas sought, and the formats of materials included. The gift policy also states that donations require the enactment of a legal deed of gift between the donor and the library, that donor requested access restrictions must be time sensitive, and that the deed identifies all copyright owners. The legal transfer of donations and copyrights is discussed more thoroughly in Chapter 3.

■ **Example Donation/Gift Policy** ──────────────────

See the Berkshire Athenaeum Pittsfield's Public Library, Pittsfield, MA (www.pittsfield library.org under the Library Policies & Procedures tab), Gift Policy and Local History Department: Collection Development Policy Statement.

DEACCESSIONING POLICY

When the collection focus changes, some types of materials previously acquired might no longer be appropriate. In order to discuss deaccessioning, we must first discuss accessioning. Public librarians probably view accessions as acquisitions and deaccessioning as weeding; archivists use the terms accessioning and deaccessioning. Both are correct and serve almost the same purpose. Archival accessioning is also the first step in creating access to archival and manuscript materials acquired for the local history archive. These procedures are discussed in Chapter 3.

Another help in understanding the similarities and differences in the terms used by librarians and archivists is Bastian, Sniffin-Marinoff, and Webber in *Archives in Libraries: What Librarians and Archivists Need to Know to Work Together*. In "Table 2. Same World, Different Meaning," a term is listed along with its archives meaning and its library meaning. For example, consider the term "accession." The archives meaning reads, "Materials physically and legally transferred to a repository as a unit at a single time; an acquisition; may involve a donor." The library meaning reads, "Recording an addition of a bibliographic item to a library collection. This addition could be acquired in a variety of ways—by purchase, gift, or exchange."[5]

The decision to deaccession collections needs to be stated as part of the collection development policy. What materials might be considered for deaccessioning? One example would be a policy that includes a statement about future changes to the local history archive collecting focus, which might create review or reappraisal of collections for deaccessioning. Cautious wording is important, however, to avoid creating uncertainty among donors and potential donors. Will deaccessioned unique items be returned to donors or, with the permission of donors, offered to other collections? What is the review procedure for deaccessioning? A statement regarding deaccessioning within the deed of gift form alerts donors to deaccessioning possibilities.

■ **Examples Deaccessioning Policy** ─────────────────

See: SAA Standards Portal, Appraisal and Acquisition (www.archivists.org/standards). The "Guidelines for Reappraisal and Deaccessioning" also includes forms and a template for writing a deed of gift with language addressing the possibility of deaccessioning.

RESOURCE SHARING/COOPERATIVE POLICY

Overlap will occur in some manner with other libraries and collections. A county historical society will contain materials similar to those in the public library local history archive. Cooperative agreements are important to assist repositories with collecting, as well as public relations. Family papers can, for example, contain the papers of politicians, academicians, scientists, women, African Americans, Chinese Americans, religious leaders, and teachers. Family papers can also contain records of businesses and organizations, and can cover numerous time periods and places. The public library local history archive, the county historical society, and the regional university could agree that only one institution will accept the papers of a certain novelist, even though she had connections to all three. Cooperative policies can state that, although an archival or manuscript collection focuses on a certain time period, the papers of a specific individual will not be collected because another library already has an extensive focus on the person. Of course, such agreements can take many forms and could be as simple as an agreement to inform fellow librarians/archivists of acquisitions in various fields.

Resource sharing can be a viable part of programs. If the public library, the historical society, and the university develop digitization programs to share unique resources, a wider public is reached, and each organization's users are better served. Another resource sharing project could be duplicating audiovisual items for or donating duplicate reprinted items to another collection.

■ **Examples Resource Sharing/Cooperative Policy** ─────────

Yakima County Heritage is coordinated by Yakima Valley Libraries, which digitizes resources from its own archives and also works with local heritage organizations to digitize and provide enhanced access to their historical collections. If you have corrections or additional details regarding records in the collection, please use the digital collection's public comments feature, or contact Yakima Valley Libraries directly to update the information (www.washingtonruralheritage.org).

POLICY IMPLEMENTATION AND REVIEW

Write procedures that indicate what staff will and will not do in regard to gifts, purchases, exhibits, special programs, research, photocopying, and liability. Of course, there are other functions that can be contained in collection development policies, but the main purpose is to give staff, administration, donors, and users guidelines for carrying out the policy.

A built-in continuous evaluation as part of the total program operation can detect any imbalance between objectives and policies. Create a time framework for review. In order to determine the effectiveness of the collection policy, at the end of each fiscal year, review the acquisitions, user records, and deaccessions of the preceding fiscal year. Staff, administrators, and even users can determine if the mission of the archive is being served through regular evaluation of accessions. The collection development policy will be reevaluated and changed as needed to meet the goals of the public library's local history archive.

Collection development policies lay the foundation. On this foundation are built the physical and intellectual control of materials in the local history archive. Chapter 3 details the six basic steps necessary to gain control of archives and manuscripts, from acquiring them to making them accessible.

NOTES

1. American Library Association, "Guidelines for the Formulation of Collection Development Policies," in Wallach John Bonk and Rose Mary Magrill, eds., *Building Library Collections*, 5th ed. (Metuchen, NJ: Scarecrow Press, 1979), 363–368. See also "Collection Development Policy Template" in Marquis and Waggener, *Local History Reference Collections for Public Libraries*, 115–122.
2. Faye Phillips, "Developing Collecting Policies for Manuscript Collections," *American Archivist*, 47 (Winter 1984): 31, 36; Dearstyne, *Managing Historical Records Programs*, 71–72.
3. Robert A. Cooke, "Managing Change in Organizations," in Gerald Zaltman, ed., *Management Principles for Nonprofit Agencies and Organizations* (New York: American Management Association, 1979), 156–157.
4. Linderman, "Archives in Public Libraries," 48; Yakel, *Starting an Archives*, 28; Phillips, "Developing Collecting Policies for Manuscript Collections," 39–42.
5. Bastian, Sniffin-Marinoff, and Webber, *Archives in Libraries*, 32.

CHAPTER 3

ACQUIRING AND MAKING LOCAL HISTORY COLLECTIONS ACCESSIBLE

> Access to special collections material has traditionally depended on those technical services functions that occur "behind the scenes": acquisitions, cataloging, and preservation.
>
> **–Beth M. Whittaker, "Get It, Catalog It, Promote It: New Challenges to Providing Access to Special Collections," RBM: A Journal of Rare Books, Manuscripts and Cultural Heritage**

PHYSICAL AND INTELLECTUAL control of archival and manuscript material—"processing"—consists of six basic steps:

1. Archival appraisal of collections offered to the public library local history archive.
2. Deed of gift and legal transfer to the public library local history archive.
3. Accessioning and basic control.
4. Arrangement.
5. Description.
6. Access.

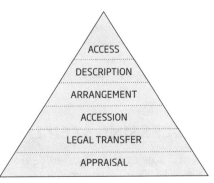

ACCESS
DESCRIPTION
ARRANGEMENT
ACCESSION
LEGAL TRANSFER
APPRAISAL

Steps 1–5 lead to Step 6: Access. Steps 3–5 are the components of archival processing, which is equivalent to original library cataloging. Original library cataloging is completed for published materials acquired by the library for which no previous record is available at www.WorldCat.org. Copying and downloading records from WorldCat is copy cataloging. Because archival and manuscript materials are unique, copy cataloging is not possible, and original cataloging is required.

■ Definitions

Processing (SAA, 314): A collective term used in archival administration that refers to the activity required to gain intellectual control of records, papers, or collections, including accessioning, arrangement, culling, boxing, labeling, description, preservation, and conservation.

Original cataloging (*ODLIS*): Preparation of a bibliographic record from scratch, without the aid of a pre-existing catalog record for the same edition, more time-consuming for the cataloger than copy cataloging.

Procedures for accomplishing these steps can vary from one local history archive to another, but the purpose for the steps remains the same—gaining legal, physical, and intellectual control of archival collections in order to preserve them and make them accessible to users.

Create a processing manual to record procedural decisions as they are made to establish consistency for the processing of future collections. An excellent example is the University of North Carolina Special Collections "Archival Processing" wiki pages (not publicly available online but contact staff at UNC for more information). Although it refers to processing functions within an academic setting, much of the manual's guidelines are adaptable to the public library local history archive. The department's processing manual can be made available to staff through a wiki page, as a file on the library's intranet, as a component of the library's web pages, and/or as a printed document. (SAA has links to processing manual pdfs.)

PROCESSING STEP 1: APPRAISAL

Local history archives often deal with two types of appraisal: tax appraisal and archival appraisal. Tax deductions for the value of gifts to the library are allowed. Gifts of family or personal papers and organizational records require an appraisal by an independent, professional appraiser not employed by the local history archive. The donor hires the appraiser and pays any fees for the appraisal. IRS rules for tax deductions can change from year to year, so donors and staff members should periodically review them at www.irs.gov.

Archival appraisal is different than tax/monetary appraisal, which estimates fair market value. It is also distinguished from the evaluation that is typically used by records managers to indicate a preliminary assessment of value using existing retention schedules. Instead, archival appraisal is the review of the materials based on the local history archive's collection development criteria to determine if the collection is acceptable for permanent preservation and is the first step in accepting archives or manuscripts. Careful planning is important, because appraisal dictates what is done next in processing, including how resources are used, how users are served, and whether or not historically valuable material is successfully preserved and accessible.

■ Definitions

Appraisal (SAA, 22): Appraisal is the process of identifying materials offered to an archive that have sufficient value to be accessioned. In an archival context, appraisal is the process of determining whether records and other materials have permanent (archival) value.

Appraisal (*ODLIS*): Appraisal refers to the process of evaluating records to determine whether they are to be archived indefinitely, retained for a shorter period, or disposed of in some other way (sold, donated, destroyed, etc.).

If possible, make an initial evaluation of the collection before physically appraising it. Collections that obviously fall outside the collection development policy do not warrant your appraisal efforts unless the potential donor has compelling proof that materials relevant to your collection policy are included among the non-relevant materials. Say no, thank you to these types of collections as soon as possible, and recommend the collection's donors/creators to an appropriate repository where the collection has a better fit. Collaborative agreements with sister institutions provide a ready list of those that might be a good home for collections not appropriate to your local history archive. Promptly decline a collection in extremely poor condition because repairing and making damaged collections user accessible requires extensive resources including staff time.

Appraisal Theory

Archival theorist and educator Richard J. Cox identifies the basic issues necessary to consider before beginning archival appraisal:

- Records are real things, whether paper or electronic.
- Personal papers, while not normally part of organizations and governments, are records nevertheless.
- All records are created for a reason, and this reason ought to have the preeminent role in their subsequent management.
- Records are essential.
- The selection of records for long-term maintenance is the key responsibility in archival and records management programs.
- "Every organization needs to manage its records to support accountability, the protection of crucial evidence, and the nurturing of corporate memory." Individuals, families, and groups also need to create records for protection, accountability, and nurturing personal memory.[1]

Administrative, legal, and fiscal values demonstrate an ongoing need by an individual, family, organization, or company to retain certain documentation for the current or future conduct of life and business. Such documentation has evidential value, and evidential records are necessary for continuing operation. Evidential value refers to the quality of the documentation about the origins, functions, and activities of the individual/family or agency/organization contained in the records (such as a birth certificate or charter) and the development and execution of major/substantive programs (such as personal financial files or minutes of the executive board). Also important is the quantity of the evidential records. Are enough records existing to understand the activities and history of the individual, the family, or the work of the agency?

Within the records are supporting, facilitative, records needed to complete functions, such as bills and receipts. Most organizational, business, and government records are facilitative (as are many personal records). These are not permanent, archival records. Bank account drafts, and checks from the 1830s might be appraised as archival for they document early banking and community developments. In addition, because of their rarity, they might hold intrinsic value, which is also looked for during archival appraisals and reviews. Intrinsic value is the inherent worth of a document based on an analysis of its age, content, usage, media, and circumstances of creation. Late nineteenth, twentieth, and twenty-first century bank checks are seldom archival.[2]

Archivists assess the informational value of records based on the usefulness or significance of the content of the materials and by projecting the possible future use of the records for reference and research. What is the scope and reliability of the data, and how much information is contained on persons, places, and events? For example, the federal census process creates records of informational value to genealogists and historians, even after those records' evidential value as a population count for the federal government has passed.[3]

What do records document about the lives of individuals and entities, the built environment, objects, and events? These questions and others are asked to determine the informational value of records. The creator, however, does not create records based on informational value. A diarist who then writes and publishes memoirs, a favorite twenty-first century genre, may be an example of an exception. An online business entrepreneur might never think of her future archives.

Archives of civic clubs, local businesses, churches, hospitals, schools, historical agencies, newspapers, libraries, and architectural firms include records that were created to accomplish the purposes of the organization. The local League of Women Voters records will contain correspondence and financial records showing how the organization functions. While current records are generally most important to the organization, archival records are valuable to researchers and for historical studies. Correspondence might contain documentation on the life of a leading citizen whose biography is being written by the county historian. Baptismal records of the local Catholic church are essential records that might have long been used by regional genealogists for their personal research. Essential records, also referred to as evidential and vital records, are those that are necessary for the ongoing business of an agency, without which the agency could not continue to function effectively. Archivists review the history of the organization and organizational charts, or the biography of the individual or family, to help make appraisal decisions. Organization charts can also be used to determine the original order of the files and establish a records management plan.

Understanding the context in which records are created is necessary for effective administrative reuse of the records by the creator or for historical use by researchers. Who created them, why were they created, how were they used, and how were they maintained?

Examples of Collection Context

Who created the records? The Jones Saddle Company CEO creates records when he corresponds with customers, the sales office creates records when they bill the customers, and the chairman of the board creates records when she prepares agendas for meetings.

Why were the records created? The Jones Saddle Company president's correspondence with customers was created for the purpose of gaining and keeping customers who buy the company's products. The sales office creates billing records to track sales and meet tax regulations and to keep contact with customers who buy the company's products. The chairmen of the board agendas are created to direct the activities of the board and establish the direction of the company's activities in creating and selling their products.

How were the records used? The Jones Saddle Company CEO's correspondence with customers is used to create an on-going link with the customer. The CEO and his office staff will refer back to the correspondence to answer questions about the customer and that customer's interaction with the company. The sales office billing of the customer records are used to track the purchasing history of the customer and meet accounting/audit requirements and tax regulations. The chairmen of the board's agendas are used as an outline of actions the board will undertake at the board meeting, such as the approval of a yearly budget.

How were the records maintained? The Jones Saddle Company CEO's correspondence is filed first chronologically by year, then by incoming letters from the customer to the CEO, alphabetically by customer name, and next by outgoing letters from the CEO to the customer, again alphabetically by customer name. The sales office records are filed by customer name for each year and then by invoice number with a cross-reference file in invoice number order. The chairmen of the board's agendas are filed yearly by date of the board meetings. Each office of the company and each board member will have copies of the agendas in their files. The context is that the Jones Saddle Company records were created in order to operate and maintain the business of making and selling saddles.

The same questions can be asked about the context of the creation of individual, family, or group papers. Personal correspondence is created to connect people, financial papers and legal documents are created to operate a family or personal life, and photographs are created and saved for remembrance and commemoration of life and activities. All of these materials can contain evidential and informational value.

Appraisal includes the recognition of records as part of an organic whole related to an organization's purpose and function, and this extends to personal records as well. A record removed from its original context among other records is difficult for users to understand and interpret. A single, unidentifiable page with your grandfather's name listed among those of other men can be a nice artifact, and it could be a census record sheet, but removed from the whole, it gives no provable documentation. In doing appraisal, archivists select the portion of the records and collections to keep. The basis for these decisions "should rest on how organizations, people, and society function," and the records preserved should serve as evidence of the functions and activities of organizations and people. Appraisal planning and policies require the archivist to know how records came to exist, while being aware that all entities who create records, albeit a person or a government, do not stand alone; they are all part of society and history. The records offered to the local history archive, no matter how extensive chronologically or physically, will always contain less than the full history of institutions, organizations, families, and individuals. Appraise records within this larger view so that the department can meet users' needs, whether the users are the original records creators, a student, or a teacher.[4]

■ Definitions

Archives (SAA, 30-32): Archives are the noncurrent records of an organization or institution preserved because of their continuing value.

Archives (*ODLIS*): An organized collection of the noncurrent records of the activities of a business, government, organization, institution, or other corporate body; a repository managed and maintained by a trained archivist; and/or an office or organization responsible for appraising, selecting, preserving, and providing access to archival materials.

Organizational and Institutional Records

Archival records of the League of Women Voters, the Rotary Club, local churches, garden clubs, the historic preservation society, lumber mills, factories, florists, morticians, newspapers, and library clubs can be acquired for the local history archive. Organizations and institutions share similar types of records. To ensure that only records of enduring value from such groups are sent to the library, "records schedules" that indicate when records should be transferred must be established. By using records schedules, permanently valuable records can be transferred to the archives and non-archival materials can be destroyed at the appropriate times. Laws govern the life cycle of some records (such as financial ones). Federal tax laws require financial records of profit and nonprofit agencies to be kept for seven years from the date of the tax statement. Correspondence and committee minutes are usually considered permanent archival records. The first point of contact for the local history archive representative varies from a staff member designated as the records manager of an organization or business, or the archives or history committee members of clubs and societies.

■ Definitions

Retention schedule (SAA, 337): A document that identifies and describes an organization's records, usually at the series level, provides instructions for the disposition of records throughout their life cycle.

Disposition schedule (*OLDIS*): A disposition schedule is a systematic list of documents used by an archivist to determine: 1) which of the recurring records of an agency or individual will be retained, 2) the period of time for which they will be held, 3) where they will be housed during the retention period (archives or intermediate storage), and 4) any other decisions concerning their disposition, based on their utility and value to the organization.

■ Example of an Organization's Records Schedule

Neighbor Village Baptist Church Records

Description of records	Retention
Deacon Board minutes	Permanent, retain in office seven years and then transfer to the public library local history archive
Church programs and publications	Retain one copy of each for the archives
Church Secretary's minutes	Permanent, retain in office seven years and then transfer to the public library local history archive
Bills and receipts	Destroy after seven years

The local history archive occasionally receives voluminous records in complete disarray and poor condition from organizations without a records management plan. Records management plans establish records schedules and designate the repository that will serve as the organizational archive. Appraisal is an essential first step before the records can be accepted. If possible, have staff do appraisal work where the records are housed, either with files already in boxes or while they are still in file cabinets and storage units.

Sorting files and/or boxes into groups of similar materials assists the appraisal process; this is one of the first steps of arrangement. Appraisal assessments help in establishing the processing priority of the potential collection within the local history archive's overall processing plan. Do not mix files being removed from filing cabinets into boxes with items from other files (such as files labeled "CEO's correspondence" with other folders labeled "committee files" and "financial records"). Brief notes about the contents of each box or other type of container should be made as each is examined or packed; these notes are kept for the collection accession file.

■ Definitions

Personal papers (SAA, 292): Personal papers are documents created, acquired, or received by an individual in the course of his or her affairs and preserved in their original order (if such order exists).

Personal papers (*ODLIS*): Personal papers are the private documents and related materials accumulated by an individual in the course of a lifetime (letters, diaries, journals, legal documents, etc.).

Personal Papers

Appraisal of individual or family papers is similar to appraisal of organizational records. Personal papers contain records just as organizational and government archives contain records. "Archivists are archivists. Archives are archives. Archives are composed of records. Historical manuscripts are composed of records, and they constitute archives. Manuscript curators are responsible for records *and* archives."

Individuals and families produce archives that are composed of their records. These records are created for the same reasons as organizational records, to create evidence of crucial work, for protection, and to provide memory.[5]

Most people have some type of workable filing system. Obtain from the creator of the papers a description of any filing systems and methods of organization used for paper files and electronic files, and maintain original order for personal papers and manuscripts, as well as for organizational records. In some cases, the original order of the papers is completely lost because of the length of time the personal records have been alienated from their creators. Correspondence, financial records, memoirs, diaries, recipe files, military papers, school records, and photographs are series found in personal papers, as well as organizational and professional files. Do not overlook computer files of the creators. Family papers given to the library naturally include the files of members who were officers of civic organizations, committee members for churches, chair people for professional groups, and leaders of children's activities such as Boy Scouts and swim teams. Family and personal papers greatly enhance the research materials in the library's local history archive.

Practice, patience, and caution are called for when appraising personal and family papers in order to identify items of enduring value. Once the appraisal is complete, return unwanted items to the owners with the stipulation that other unwanted materials might be identified and returned at a later date. Ask the donor if other unwanted items should be returned or discarded after processing.

Appraisal is a look at the entire group of records to determine what will be transferred to the archives and what will be left with the organization for eventual destruction. Arrange materials within subject categories (such as family correspondence), describe the type and format of materials, and record the dates covered. Retain original file folders with their contents, as file folder labels will be important during arrangement and description of the records. Also, retain any notes from the creator included with the records about the files or their contents. Biographical notes made during appraisal are used in writing sections of the finding aid as well as providing index terms/access points. Recent guidelines for appraisal of digital records can be found within the SAA Trends in Archives Practice *Appraisal and Acquisition Strategies* "Module 14: Appraising Digital Records" (www.archivists.org, Publications pull-down menu, Bookstore tab).

Processing steps that occur simultaneously improve efficiency. While appraising a collection, obvious physical and preservation needs (such as re-boxing when boxes are in poor condition or cleaning away dust) can be assessed and fulfilled. Also identify more subtle preservation needs, such as cassette and reel-to-reel tapes needing to be reformatted into digital files, and electronic files requiring appropriate software before users can access the information contained.

To Accept or Not to Accept

After the initial archival appraisal is completed, you will need to decide if you will accept the collection or decline it? Saying no to a potential donor of materials is never easy. Plus, you might be hesitant to decline a collection on which you've already spent time—probably even including some sorting of the materials during your archival appraisal. However, it is better to say no to the donor at this stage than to accept a collection that does not fit your local history archive's policies. Such collections might sit in the backlog unprocessed while collections that are relevant to your collection policy receive a higher processing priority. Donors, as well as library administrators, are more likely to understand the rejection of a collection directly after the appraisal process than they will understand why an accepted collection is not being publicized nor made available to users.

Even if the offered collection does not fit the current collection development policy, do the papers or records evoke a new collecting area the department, the library, and its users wish to consider? If, for example, your local history archive collects and seeks to continue to collect the papers and records of the first African American families in Everywhere County, but the collection offered documents the first African American church in a county three states west of your state, then no, do not accept this collection. If the offered collection, however, contains the papers and records of the Ladies' Sports League of Everywhere County and your users are requesting more information about local women's history, you could see this collection as a new focus area.

At this point, re-box materials if necessary and use acid-free records center cartons in preparation for transport to the library. Label boxes according to the groups/series they contain, along with the name of the donor, family or organization, and number them. Use temporary labels rather than permanent ones. Also, label the boxes to be retained by the donor, with suggested dates of destruction for organizational files. Prepare a deed of gift to be signed by the donor of personal papers and by the public library's authorized official. For organizational records, an official agreement designating the local history archive as the repository for the organization is necessary and requires the signatures of an authorized representative of both the public library and the organization. Such an agreement establishes a continuing transfer of the organization's records. After an agreement is in place, a deed of gift is also prepared to transfer physical custody. When a designated group of records is to be transferred, prepare a transfer form (also known as a records transmittal form) for signature by a representative of the organization and the library.

Each local history archive defines its appraisal criteria and devises a checklist to determine if a possible acquisition is archival. Included in the procedures manual is the appraisal criteria and how to use the checklist. Add to the manual other appraisal situations unique to the department's collection development policies. Planning is the foundation on which all other archival functions are built, so establish a processing program to define, plan, implement, assess, and evaluate the activities inherent in processing. An essential component of the processing program is to develop processing priorities that assist with decision-making about the appraisal of potential collections to be acquired, processing the backlog of previously acquired but unprocessed collections, preservation, and deaccessioning. Establish criteria for where the newly accepted collection will be placed in the processing queue. Included are the same questions asked in the appraisal checklist below, as well as questions about current research demand, anticipated research use, staff availability, and the time needed to process the collection, as well as other criteria needed by a given institution.

The local history archive will need to establish consistent processing steps to assess collections of different sizes, various contents, existing levels of arrangement, and complexity. An evaluative "processing priorities" checklist can help. It can answer questions, such as: Will the content of the collection have a high, medium or low demand by users? Does the physical condition necessitate a high, medium, or low level of preservation work? How much staff time will be required (a high amount because the collection is unorganized, low because it is well organized, or some medium amount in between)? Is there a large, medium, or small number of items that need to be reformatted (such as video tapes and digital files)?

Processing plans and establishment of planning criteria are specifically important to departments with a backlog of unprocessed collections. New local history archives can proceed by processing each new collection in the order in which it is accessioned, one after the other. However, as each new archive grows and develops its own collecting program, criteria for determining an order in which to process collections will become necessary. In year one, if three small- to medium-sized family paper collections are accessioned, it is possible that all three can be fully processed and made accessible during the same year. If however, two medium-sized family papers collections and 100 feet of archival records from the Jones Saddle Company are accessioned in the department's second year of operation, which will be processed first and why? In its third year, the local history archive might acquire an addition to the Jones Saddle Company Records. Will this addition be processed before or after the processing of other collections received that year and why? The criteria you've established for the processing plan guides your decisions.

■ Appraisal Checklist Worksheet* Example

Sample appraisal questions. Depending upon the local history archive's guidelines, a certain percentage of the answers must be yes for the collection to be accepted as a new accession (such as 50 percent or more). Add questions to the appraisal checklist as needed and approved.

Review the collection to determine the following before accepting an acquisition:

1. Do the materials fit within the current collection development policy?
2. Does the collection represent a new collecting area the local history archive wishes to add to its collection development policy?
3. Are the materials in good to excellent condition?

If yes, a collection fits the collecting policy, but if the materials are heavily damaged, the resources required to preserve them might preclude its acquisition. Exceptions could exist because of the rarity of materials within the collection.

4. Do procedures exist for maintaining and making accessible all formats of materials represented?
5. What formats of materials are included (loose paper, photographs, maps, notebooks, diaries, drawings, postcards, audio-visual items, etc.)? Are electronic records and digital files included?
6. Do the materials cover a significant portion of the individual's life, the family's existence in the local area, or the organization's existence?
7. What is the completeness of the collection? Is the collection complete enough to be valuable for patron use?
8. Will the physical size of the collection overwhelm the available staff, the supply budget, and/or the department's storage size?
9. Is the donor asking for any unreasonable restrictions on access to the materials?
10. Does the collection contain files that are protected by the Federal Privacy Act (such as student or medical records)?
11. Based on your appraisal, can you place the collection in the processing queue at an established level of high, medium, or low priority?

*Hackbart-Dean and Slomba, *How to Manage Processing*, 35, 68–69.

Recap: Conducting an Appraisal, How to Do It

1. *If the materials offered do not fit the scope of the collection development policy, decline the collection. The only action needed is a polite letter to the owner declining the offer.* If the materials do fit the scope of the collection development policy, physically review the materials where the

collection is located (donor's offices or home). If there is not sufficient space at that location, bring the materials to the local history archive workspace, but only if the condition of the material warrants further review. Do not accept collections with mold, extensive insect damage, torn and discolored paper, and bad odors. Most local history archives have limited funds for restoration of such items. Some dirt, dust, and insect remains are manageable and can be dealt with in order to save a valuable collection.

2. *In an appropriate space with worktables and archival tools, open boxes, bags, and other containers to review the order—or lack of order—within them. A collection with a discernable order is easily reviewed with the appraisal checklist and a decision can be efficiently made. If an order is not apparent, sort files as they relate to the same activity or function, and/ or by the person, organization, or office that created or compiled them.* Create appraisal notes at each step. If you prefer to handwrite notes, keep them together in the same place as you finish working on each collection. If you prefer to use a computer, name the file so that you can always locate it. Good housekeeping of your appraisal notes is critical. When conducting an appraisal of files still in file cabinets, do not box the materials until you are sure the collection will be accepted. For collections in boxes, if your appraisal is positive and the collection will be accessioned, decide if boxes need replacing before transporting them. Replace any boxes that are split, water damaged, smashed at the corners, smelly, or covered with confusing labels and markings. Use archival boxes. If files are in records center boxes or commercial moving boxes and are in good condition, keep the files and folders in those boxes; do not replace the boxes at this time. Replace folders only if they are severely damaged. Any loose documents should be placed into folders. Further housing of the collection will be done during arrangement.

3. Moving appraised and accepted collections to the local history archive:

    A. For personal papers, prepare a deed of gift. In most cases, it is preferable not to move any collections until the deed of gift is signed by both the donor and the appropriate public library official. After the deed is signed (or if the safety of the collection requires that it be moved before the deed is signed) prepare a receipt for the donor. The donor's signature on the receipt authorizes you to move the collection.

    B. For organizational records appraised as acceptable, and for which the organization and public library have an authorized agreement and a deed of gift, prepare a transmittal form for the materials to be moved. This form is the official receipt that authorizes you to move the materials.

C. Prepare a shipping list (even if library staff members are moving the collection), and check each box off the shipping list as it arrives and is unloaded at the library. Commercial moving firms authorized to contract with the library can be hired to move collections from out of town. The library business office handles the contracts, and the commercial firm provides their version of shipping lists. Be sure the moving firms lists meet the library's and the donor's requirements.

4. When the collection arrives at the library, review all shipping lists during the unloading of materials. Based on condition issues found during the appraisal, determine if insect control is needed, and follow the library's and local history archive's procedures for that. Having adequate space as a holding area for new accessions is often a luxury; however, if possible, designate such an area. Shelve new collections, and indicate the locations of all local history archive records related to the collection (such as appraisal notes, box labels, in-house databases, and the accession register). Place each collection in the processing queue or processing priority list.

5. Proceed to Processing Step 2: Legal Transfer.

PROCESSING STEP 2: LEGAL TRANSFER

Collections appraised as acceptable for acquisition must be legally transferred to the library. Privately owned collections are transferred through a deed of gift—a formal, legal document. Physical and legal custody is transferred to the public library as a collection within the local history archive. The deed or agreement also must specify who holds copyright to the gift. Some donors retain intellectual rights and copyrights to the collection and transfer only the property/physical rights. Copyrights to individual items within the collection remain the property of the creator (such as the writer of a letter), and are not the property of the recipient of the letter. If a copyright is to be transferred later upon the death of a donor, the name and contact of the future holder should be included. Clearly state bequests requested by donors and accepted by the local history archive.

Deed of Gift

Public libraries are required to follow the rules and laws of the city, county, and state governments to which it belongs. Entering into legal agreements might not be the purview of the administrator of the local history archive or even of the library director. Donations of any type to the public library require proper and legal approval, either by the library director, the public library board of directors, or others such as the city's legal department. The wording of any deed of gift used by the public library should follow a template established and approved by the official parties. When a collection is given, the archivist/librarian fills in the appropriate information specifically related to the potential gift and submits it to library administration for approval. A public library might require the archivist/librarian to answer questions from its board of directors or legal department before the gift is approved. It is not unusual for a local history archive to work with an acquisitions committee as the first step in approving gifts. The final deed of gift requires the signatures of both the donor as well as an official authority as required and ordained by the public library director and local government.

If the local history archive is a new department, the archivist/librarian has an opportunity to influence procedures and the content of forms and templates for a deed of gift. However, even if all procedures regarding gifts are set and a required template for writing a deed of gift is in place, all staff members benefit from knowledge of the procedures and the legal aspects.

■ Definitions

Deed of gift (SAA, 108-109): An agreement transferring title to property without an exchange of monetary compensation. In archives, deeds of gift frequently take the form of a contract establishing conditions governing the transfer of title to documents and specifying any restrictions on access and use.

Deed of gift (*ODLIS*): A signed document stating the terms of agreement under which legal title to real, personal, or intellectual property, such as a gift of materials to a library or archives, is transferred, voluntarily and without recompense, by the donor to the recipient institution, with or without conditions.

Deeds of gift are in the best interest of both donor and repository for they establish and govern the legal relationship of each and the legal status of the materials, and define future access, ownership, and use of the collections. A deed of gift is a formal contract and is binding on the parties who have entered into it. If the local history archive fails to meet its obligations, the contract can be voided and the items reclaimed by the donor. Everyone assumes responsibility for the personal understanding of all parts of the agreement before signing. The Society of American Archivists (www2.archivists.org) has compiled "A Guide to Deeds of Gift" brochure, available on their website under the tab About Archives.[6] The Society of Georgia Archivists (www.soga .org) forms web page contains sample deeds of gift. The East Baton Rouge Parish Library Baton Rouge Room provides information about donating personal papers in a brochure.

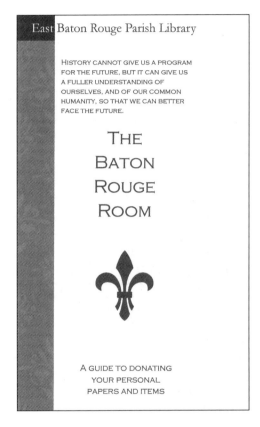

East Baton Rouge Parish Library

HISTORY CANNOT GIVE US A PROGRAM FOR THE FUTURE, BUT IT CAN GIVE US A FULLER UNDERSTANDING OF OURSELVES, AND OF OUR COMMON HUMANITY, SO THAT WE CAN BETTER FACE THE FUTURE.

THE
BATON
ROUGE
ROOM

A GUIDE TO DONATING
YOUR PERSONAL
PAPERS AND ITEMS

FIGURE 3.1

Guidance in a brochure for donors to the Baton Rouge Room.

Courtesy of the East Baton Rouge Parish Library.

■ The Elements of a Typical Deed of Gift

- The name of the donor as well as the donor's relationship to the creator of the records, if different.
- The name of the recipient. For example, is the gift being donated to the local history archive, the public library, or to the governing body (i.e., the city or state)?
- The date of the transfer of title.
- Details about the materials conveyed by the deed of gift (such as the creator of the items, the volume, inclusive dates, and general description).

- The transfer of rights to the physical and intellectual property. The name of the person or institution holding copyright as well as the time period covered under copyright (based on copyright law). If the copyright will be passed to others through planned inheritance, the heirs and their contact information are also included.
- A statement of restrictions on use. Typically there is a time restriction or a content restriction (confidential materials are closed). Specify who can impose restrictions, to what materials the restrictions apply, who can lift restrictions, and how someone requests a temporary waiver of restrictions.
- Disposal criteria and authority. Under what circumstances are materials disposed of, if they are duplicates, if they do not have historical value, or if they do not fit the acquisitions' policy or areas of collecting? If the local history archive does not retain part of the collection, what are the options (return items to the donor, transfer them to other repositories, or destroy them)? State also that these options apply if and when other items not appropriate to the local history archive are identified.*

*Hunter, Developing and Maintaining Practical Archives, 90–93.

Online auctions such as eBay and TV programs such as *Antiques Roadshow* and *Genealogy Roadshow* naturally create curiosity about the possible value of family papers and other materials. A family descendant might appear in your office asking you to return to him donations made by his ancestors. In such an instance, a signed, formal deed of gift proves ownership. Diplomacy could turn the incident from confrontation to education. Show him or her the collection donated by the ancestors, and explain how it is used, the environmental protection and security applied to every item, and the time and expense spent on the collection. Hopefully by the end of the tour, because of the care provided to his ancestor's materials, the visitor might come to realize the importance of keeping the collection within the archive, and perhaps he or she might even have other materials to add to it.

Organizational Agreement

An institution, organization, club, church, or non-profit agency can designate a local history archive as the repository for its records. Active organizations that deposit records often retain all ownership rights to those records. For organizational records, an official agreement designating the local history archive as the repository for the organization is necessary and requires signatures of an authorized representative of both the public library and the organization. Such an agreement presumes continuing transfer of the organization's records and that records created or compiled in the course of business will be transferred at the appropriate time. After an agreement is in place, a deed of gift is also prepared for the organization to transfer physical custody and if desired, any intellectual rights. If the organization ceases to function, then complete legal ownership of the records can be transferred to the local history archive.

■ An example of a first paragraph of an organization's agreement with the local history archive*

Jones Saddle Company hereby designates the Everytown Public Library Local History Archive as the official repository for the Company.

The Jones Saddle Company Board of Directors authorizes the General Manager to implement the agreement and oversee transmittal of archival materials to the Everytown Public Library annually.

Under the direction of the General Manager in conjunction with the manager of the Local History Archive, appropriate records schedules shall be established.

Company staff shall follow the records schedules to identify archival materials to be transferred.

*This is not intended to be construed as legal advice. Attorneys for the organization and the public library will, of course, write the agreement following established procedures.

Records Transmittal Form

Local history archive personnel can work with groups whose records they wish to collect to establish records schedules and a proper records management plan. When files are ready to be moved, the organization and archivist/librarian use a transmittal form that serves as a receipt for the records transferred and as a listing of the files. The authorized persons sign transmittal forms. The existence of confidential materials, any restrictions, and the availability of the records for research (i.e., upon receipt in the local history archive, after preliminary processing, or not until all processing is completed) are noted. After records with a completed transfer form are received, they are accessioned. Legal agreements, such as organizational agreements designating the local history archive as the official archives, transmittal forms, and the deed of gift, are printed for official signatures, and the signed originals are then stored in the collection/donor files. A security file of scans of the documents can also be stored in backup electronic records. When the records of a defunct organization are donated, the department's standard appraisal criteria is followed to determine if the organization's records will be accepted.

■ What to include on a records transmittal form*

- The official name of the entity transferring records. Although the records transferred might be from the grants and contracts office, the official entity might be, for example, the Everywhere County Board of Education. The division name, such as Grants and Contracts Office, would be listed separately.
- Date of transmittal.
- Name of division/department/office.
- Name of contact person and contact information.
- The type of records transferred. For the grants and contracts office, this could include correspondence with grant agencies and copies of grant applications. For the president's office, this could include Board of Directors meeting minutes.
- Estimated volume.
- Restrictions required and to whom the restrictions apply. For example, access might be closed to researchers until the records are processed to ensure that all student identification files, as required by federal law, have been removed.
- Signatures of authorizing officials from the organization and the library.**

*This is not intended to be construed as legal advice.
**Some archivists/librarians prefer to use standardized forms. Examples are available at the Society of Georgia Archivists Form Forum website (www.soga.org under the Quick Links tab).

Include the appraisal report on the collection, the signed original deed of gift and/or official transmittal form, correspondence with donors and library administrators, copies of wills or bequests, and any other relevant documentation (such as newspaper clippings about the collection or donors) in donor files as the permanent records of the local history archive. Traditionally, these donor/collection files were papers compiled in file cabinets in the administrative offices, and eventually included the accession form, a printed copy of finding aids to the collection, letters from researchers about the collection, and continuing correspondence with donors, as well as deeds or transmittal records for additions to the collection. These accession files are mostly electronic in the twenty-first century, but it is recommended that signed, original legal documents be kept on paper, while keeping electronic scans as further backup. The local history archive administrator can assign a staff person the responsibility of maintaining up-to-date legal agreements, as well as periodically reviewing and updating contact information for heirs.

Monetary Appraisals for Donors

Since the value of their gift to the public library—a non-profit agency—can be used as a federal income tax deduction, donors often ask for an appraisal. However, appraisals done by local history archive staff are not acceptable to the IRS; thus, donors must employ an independent appraiser. The department can, however, maintain a list of qualified appraisers that they provide to donors when requested. Because donor tax appraisals are required in the year in which the donation was completed, a gift consisting of a large collection requiring preliminary processing strains staff resources. If possible, briefly review a collection before the appraiser sees it. Professional appraisers should be treated as users working under the same access rules as other researchers.

Donor Requested Restrictions

Donors do request restrictions, and local history archives have an ethical and practical responsibility to accept them. However, the staff must be cautious about accepting unreasonable restrictions, especially permanent ones. If donors place restrictions on gifts, this information is contained in the deed or agreement. Limit restrictions to a short period of time, and do not accept the collection if the local history archive cannot meet the requirements of the restrictions. Even a collection that fits the research needs of users must be rejected if, for example, a donor requests permanent exhibition of the items in the collection. Few public libraries have the luxury of space for permanent exhibitions. Also, permanently exhibiting archives and manuscripts items is poor preservation practice. Gifts that donors wish closed to research for longer than the lifetimes of identified persons represented in the collection can also be an unmanageable request and limits the value of the collection.

Restrictions apply to time or content of the materials or both as needed. A donor can request that certain correspondence be closed or that all papers be closed until his or her death. Whatever the restrictions, clearly state them in the deed of gift or transfer document so that current and future staff, the donor, and the donor's family understand all agreements related to restrictions. A donor can also request that materials in his or her papers that might be found offensive to living persons be closed for a set period of time and request archivists to identify such materials during processing. Staff must be careful that the donor's heirs do not construe restrictions to mean that normal archival work on the restricted materials may not be performed. A donor's desire to approve research requests for the use of donated materials is not acceptable. Limited closure of materials that the owner finds sensitive is an alternative to permanent restrictions. When a donor retains copyrights to materials, users will have to request permission to publish directly from the donor. Donors need to understand this obligation.

Organizations and institutions depositing their records in the local history archive occasionally request restrictions to access as well. Current financial records and records of ongoing court cases should be maintained by the donor organization, but not transferred. Files of settled lawsuits and minutes of closed board meetings can be transferred, but restricted. Files can be closed in compliance with the wishes of the donating organizations and the law.

Librarians/archivists will find themselves faced with requirements of the Federal Privacy Act and other relevant state and local laws. Personal details, such as those included in medical, legal, or congressional case files, cannot be legally released to users without permission from the individual, nor can information supplied to fulfill legal requirements (driver's license or marriage license applications, for example) be available to users for research. However, this information may be used for statistical purposes, as long as specific names or identifiable information are not divulged. Laws about defamation and the right to privacy must be observed and access to records restricted accordingly.

Abandoned or Orphaned Collections

Deaccessioning might need to be used for abandoned or orphaned collections. In some cases, materials might have been deposited in the local history archive without a deed of gift being executed; therefore, clear ownership is not evident. Such collections might have also been accessioned. Following the abandoned property guidelines of the Society of American Archivists, the department will make every reasonable attempt to contact the person who delivered the materials to the library. If no response is received after a designated time period (say, for example, three months), materials will be either deaccessioned or accepted as the property of the library. Deaccessioned material that are not claimed can be offered to another, more appropriate library.

In 2009, the Society of American Archivists published a report of its Abandoned Property Project Committee. The Abandoned Property in Cultural Institutions Law Project is an effort to identify states that have laws that allow cultural institutions such as museums and archives to obtain ownership of abandoned or orphan collections, loaned property in the possession of a repository for which the repository has no reasonable means of contacting its owner.[7] The East Baton Rouge Parish Library's Baton Rouge Room has established a policy based on the statements recommended by the SAA Committee.

■ Abandoned Property Policy Example

From time to time, archival collections and items are loaned to the Baton Rouge Room archives. Occasionally, these collections go unclaimed. The East Baton Rouge Parish Library will assume ownership of the items if the following qualifications are met:

- The East Baton Rouge Parish Library has held the property for three or more years.
- The East Baton Rouge Parish Library sends notice by certified mail, return receipt requested, to the last known address of the lender.
- If the collection is undocumented (that is, if the name of the original owner is unknown), the East Baton Rouge Parish Library publishes a notice in the local newspaper where it is located.

If no response is received after three months, the collection is considered abandoned and becomes property of the East Baton Rouge Parish Library.

Recap: Legal Transfer, How to Do It

1. Receipt of a collection from an individual, family, or group of individuals: Draft a deed of gift based on your discussions and agreements with the donors. Include any required and agreed upon restrictions to access, and identify those individuals that hold copyrights to the materials in the collection, either as a whole or in part. Present a draft of the deed of gift to the public library official responsible for legal agreements, and with the official's authorization, submit the draft to the donor. Make any required changes to the draft, and finalize the deed of gift with proper signatures.
2. Receipt of a collection from an organization, institution, agency, etc.: If the donor organization is still functioning and plans to donate future installments of their records, ask that the governing body approve the local history archive as the archival repository for the organization. The public library official responsible for legal agreements must also approve. Prepare a transfer form for the first installment of the records. Each subsequent accrual will also require a transfer form. If the donor organization is defunct, then follow the next steps as outlined in point 1 (receipt from an individual).

3. Create a "Donor File" for the collection and combine all local history archive generated notes and forms with the legal deeds or agreements. This is a permanent record of local history archive acquisitions.
4. Update administrative and donor files.
5. Proceed to Processing Step 3: Accessioning.

PROCESSING STEP 3: ACCESSIONING

Acquiring proper items for the local history archive in public libraries, based on collection evaluation and collection development policies, can be accomplished through gifts, purchases, bequests, and deposits. Individuals and families might be sources of materials, and organizations might transfer their archival records.

■ Definitions

Accession (SAA, 3): Materials physically and legally transferred to a repository as a unit at a single time; an acquisition. To take legal and physical custody of a group of records or other materials and to formally document their receipt in a register, database, or other log of the repository's holdings.

Accession (*ODLIS*): In archives, the formal act of accepting and documenting the receipt of records taken into custody, part of the process of establishing physical and intellectual control over them. In the case of donated items, a deed of gift may be required to transfer legal title.

Archival and manuscript materials appraised as acceptable to be acquired will be legally transferred to the public library and accessioned. The purpose of accessioning is to enable the department staff to gain immediate physical and intellectual control over the contents of collections. An accession register that lists accessions and their locations provides inventory control for the entire local history archive. Books and other printed materials purchased as sets or one at a time by the public library are also accessioned. Capabilities of the acquisitions module of the library's ILS (integrated library system) can often be used to accession archives and manuscripts. If it is not possible to utilize the ILS, an accession register can be created in a simple spreadsheet format or a database. Archival management software programs, which are separate from the ILS, also provide accession functions. Accession procedures include assigning all accepted collections a unique and permanent identifying number in a continuous, chronological order of receipt, such as 001 to 1000. This number 001 indicates the first accession out of a total of 1,000 accessions. Many departments add an additional number to indicate the year (for example, 001–16 through 999–16, 001–2016 through 999–2016, or 2016:001). Each year, accession numbers begin again (for example, 001–17 or 001–2017, or 2017:001). Over time, additional materials—sometimes unexpected—will be added to previously accessioned collections. An effective accessioning system utilizing two collection numbers alleviates confusion. The first accession number for the Jones Saddle Company Records is 2016:001, and it is assigned the collection number 0701. More records from the Jones Saddle Company are received and accessioned as numbers 2017:005 and 2018:022. These are additions/accretions to the collection and are connected by the same collection number (0701). The record shows how many additions were received and accessioned through the years. Even if additions to a collection's first accession are not anticipated, assigning a collection number in addition to the accession number gives the local history archive an extra level of control.

Accession records contain basic information about the collections that is represented by each accession number. The accession record will provide: the accession number and the collection number; the collection's title, its origin, and its creator; and the content, format, and extent of the materials. It is at this point that the collection will receive an appropriate name or title. Notes taken during appraisal about processing needs, plans, and priorities are reviewed and revised as needed. Preliminary sorting and cleaning, if necessary, are done or continued from work begun during appraisal. All unlabeled containers receive temporary identification labels. Once these steps are completed, staff members find suitable storage for the new accession.

Prepare an accession worksheet for each new accession and each addition to a previously accessioned collection. Integrated library systems and archives management software use the MARC (Machine Readable Cataloging) format to create records within their systems. Users find collections through the MARC records in the library's online catalog. "MARC is a numeric data structure for bibliographic description, authority, classification, and holdings data that is utilized for describing bibliographic materials. It is also used to facilitate cooperative cataloging and data exchange between integrated library systems." WorldCat (www.worldcat.org) is a worldwide database that includes access records for millions of items and collections in multiple formats (not just published books). Not all public libraries submit information on their holdings to WorldCat, but those that do have their holdings information available continuously.

Archives and manuscript collections can be included in WorldCat by utilizing data from the accession worksheet correlated with MARC record identifiers. (See the following example.) An accession worksheet can be the first access point for users of the local history archive and can serve as a temporary finding aid until the appropriate level of arrangement and description is completed. Each entry, date of receipt, name of collection, inclusive dates, etc., is correlated with a MARC tag; for example, in MARC the tag number 245 is the title information. A note stating that the collection is unprocessed or partially processed but is open for users helps bring new accessions to the users quickly.[8] A public library's technical services or cataloging team will be able to assist the local history archive in preparing MARC tagged accession sheets adapted to the individual library's procedures.

Many ILS software-cataloging modules permit a so-called "Easy MARC" bibliographic entry that is indeed easy to use accurately with proper training. Using common tools and descriptive standards reduces costs and provides better access. Also important to facilitate searching of archives and manuscript collections is the use of standardized vocabulary data, such as the Library of Congress Subject Headings' authority files (https://authorities.loc.gov). These are used with "MARC21" entries. Library of Congress Authorities are used nationally. So, for example, if your Seattle local history archive holds a collection created by Ernest Hemingway, you would use the standardized form established by LC for a collection in the Seattle Public Library.

■ Accession Worksheet Correlated with "MARC21" Example ──

099 (control number, local identifier) Accession number:	Date of receipt/accessioned:
245a, b (title statement)	Title of collection:
100	Personal name:
110	Corporate name:
561 (provenance)	Name and address of source/donor:
Description of collection (approximate volume, inclusive dates, and general subject matter)	
245f	Inclusive dates:
245g	Bulk dates:
300	Physical description (volume)

351	Arrangement/organization:
545	Biographical/historical note:
520	Scope and content note:
540	Restrictions/terms governing use:
650	Subject added entry–topical term:
651	Subject added entry–geographical:
700	Personal name as added entry:
710	Corporate name as added entry:
600	Personal name as subject:
610	Corporate name as subject:

Comments/Notes:

Status: ____gift ____deposit _____ bequest ____ transfer

Donor e-mail and telephone number:

Processing Plan:

Priority in processing queue: _____high _____medium _____low

In *Managing Historical Records Programs,* Dearstyne presents examples of how to use MARC tags for accession records, and in *Developing and Maintaining Practical Archives,* Hunter lists some of the most important fields for archival description. This format provides a standard set of accession file information elements to be gathered for collections and placed in the library database and the local history archive's accession register. In *Organizing Archival Records,* Carmicheal presents sample accession sheets explaining the elements to be included.[9] Much of the information compiled about each collection during appraisal fits within elements of the accession worksheet, and of course, the identification of donors and their rights to the collections, as well as donor-imposed restrictions, will appear again in legal transfer documents. Each of the various steps of processing builds one upon the other until access is reached. It is not necessary to start over at each step—only to combine elements as you progress.

In Scenario A (see page 21) Jane Doe, the Local History Librarian, is confronted with materials that were collected or deposited before she arrived. She is now trying to gain control over these unaccessioned collections. Jane has established accessioning procedures for the archives and manuscript collections received during her time at the Everytown Public Library. James Dotson in Scenario B (see page 23) has similar unaccessioned archives and manuscript collections in the Neighbor Village Public Library Local History Archive. When he first began working, he located a list of collections identified by title, each with an assigned, unique number. To James, this represents an accession register and a level of control over the collections listed. How do Jane Doe and James Dotson proceed to gain control over the unaccessioned collections?

They can begin by grouping the items by names of people that, despite appearing in various ways, seem to represent the creators of the materials. Create a collection for which the identification of the donor is lost; for example, accession a scrapbook from the Rivers Family, along with photographs of and sermons written by Rev. Tom Rivers, as the Rev. Tom Rivers Papers. Jane finds a letter written on April 16, 1960, from the Everytown Public Library Director to Oscar Rivers, thanking him for giving Rev. Rivers' sermons to the library. Jane uses this letter to date the donation of the collection "April 1960" and assigns and applies the accession number 2016:028 in June 2016. In the collections register at the Neighbor Village Public Library, James finds a 1905 entry under Smith Family donation with the number 0004. He uses this to create an accession worksheet for the Smith Family Papers, received in 1905 and numbered 1905:0004. Jane and James include their descriptions of the contents found that could be considered the Rev. Tom Rivers Papers in the Everytown Local History Archive and the Smith Family Papers in the Neighbor Village Local History Archive. Finally, they prioritize these collections for processing. Both find small groups of materials and some single items that they could not easily associate with any one family or person. Jane creates a collection of Rivers Family Letters and accessions them with the accession number 2016:043. She notes on the accession record and in the register that she created this collection in October 2016.

The archivist/librarian can search through the department and library files for any documentation on unaccessioned collections. Perhaps the library director wrote a thank-you letter to someone who left a group of materials for the local history archive. Library annual reports often list yearly gifts and identify donors. If the library issued newsletters, look for bits of information about the collections. Create accession records using the information found, if any. When faced with loose materials with no information about what they are or how they came to the library, try to group materials by the possible creator or compiler. The last resort is to group materials together by format such as scrapbooks, unidentified correspondence, ledgers, etc., and sometimes ephemera that you will house in vertical files. Each artificial—though reluctant— collection can be accessed as such.

Deaccessioning

Public libraries practice weeding based on policies and procedures. Books are periodically removed from the circulating collection because of condition, age, lack of relevance, being superseded by other editions, etc. Purchased items are the property of the public library and its local government. Archival and manuscript materials acquired and accessioned by the local history archive are also the property of the public library and its local government, based on the deeds of gift. The removal of accessioned materials is defined as deaccessioning.

■ Definitions

Deaccessioning (SAA, 107): Materials may be deaccessioned because they have been [archivally] reappraised and found to be no longer suitable for continuing preservation. Materials that are badly decomposed and beyond repair may be deaccessioned. Deaccessioned materials may be offered back to its donor, offered to another institution, or destroyed. Also called *permanent withdrawal.*

Deaccession (*ODLIS*): The process of deleting from an accession record documents and other materials that are to be removed from a library collection. Also refers to any item so removed. The opposite of accession. In archives, the process of removing records or documents from official custody, undertaken after careful consideration, usually as the result of a decision to transfer the material to another custodian or because the legal owner desires its return or the material is found upon reappraisal to be of doubtful authenticity or inappropriate for the collection. Synonymous with *permanent withdrawal.*

Once deaccessioned, the collections are removed from the accession records, and inventories of the collections are removed from public access, as are online information and records in the ILS.

Final disposition decisions are also based on policies and procedures. If a deed of gift exists for a collection, review it to ascertain if the donor asked for return of unwanted items. Be cautious about donors who have taken a tax credit for their gift to the library, for if they have, materials cannot be returned to them. The deaccessioned materials could be donated to another local history archive whose collecting policy includes the types of items in the collection or has a subject collecting area that fits the deaccessioned collection. Items could be sold through a Friends of the Library auction or a books and materials sale.

Processing Plan

During Appraisal Processing (Step 1), the checklist determines whether or not a collection will be acquired. If the collection fits the collecting policy, the formats and overall condition of the collection are reviewed. The answers to these condition and format questions will allow an analysis of resources required to process the collection. The size, complexity, and reformatting needs of the collection also factor into the analysis. Another processing decision that must be included in the resources analysis is the inclusion of a possible digital project component in the collection's processing. The processing plan is developed based on the policies and procedures followed for all planning activities. Clear and achievable objectives are required. After accessioning, review whether or not the processing priority level you assigned to the collection during appraisal requires revision or can remain the same.

What's in a Name?

How do you determine the tile of the collection? Why does it matter? Please refer back to Scenarios A and B (see pages 21–24). The Everytown Public Library Local History Archive's largest collection is the one created by several members of the Rivers family in the nineteenth century and was donated by the great-grandchildren of Rev. Rivers. Included are materials from the family's hardware store. These are intellectually identified as manuscripts and would be titled "Rivers Family Papers." The local history archive's second largest collection is the Everywhere County Cattle Ranchers Association office files, which were donated in 2016 by the still active association. These are intellectually identified as archives, are non-current organizational files, and are titled the Everywhere County Cattle Ranchers Association Records. A book titled *Smith Family Archives*, authored by Jason Smith, and printed and published by A. Smith Editions, Inc., is not cataloged as archives or manuscripts, but instead as a published book by established cataloging rules. A box of correspondence belonging to the Smith Family, including letters written to Jason Smith and letters to the editor at A. Smith Editions, Inc., is not cataloged as a book nor given a call number; it is a box of manuscripts properly titled "Smith Family Papers."

This chapter is about principles and accepted practices for the arrangement and description of archives and manuscripts and accurate naming is required for proper access. Naming and identification are also important for answering ownership and copyright questions, and maintaining security.

Provenance and original order are the first principles to be used in naming or giving a title to materials. Provenance means that files and materials created, assembled, accumulated, and/or maintained and used by an organization, individual, or family are kept together and not physically mixed or combined with the files of another organization, individual or family. The files and materials are physically arranged and intellectually described in their original order. Sometimes it is not possible to determine who created or compiled the collection; therefore, name the collection for the person who is the subject of the collection. For example, because Joseph Smith signed all the drawings in a group, he is the person most closely associated with the collection; thus, the collection is named "Joseph Smith Drawings Collection," even though it is not known who collected the drawings and placed them in the library.[10]

Archives are the permanently valuable, noncurrent records of organizations, businesses, institutions, and governments. The archives of the organization or institution's divisions are known as record groups. Archives are also the agency responsible for selecting, preserving, and making available records determined to have permanent or continuing value (such as the Rockefeller Foundation Archives). A building where an archival institution or special collection is located can also be called archives (such as the Louisiana State Archives). The records of institutions, organizations, and local government will often cause archives and manuscript collections to overlap. For example, a person might give papers that contain business records of the family's lumber mill and personal correspondence among family members, as well as printed and non-printed items. Correct naming and proper finding aids can sort through such overlap for researchers.

Recap: Accessioning, How to Do It

1. Look over your appraisal notes.
2. Gather the basic information to fill out the accession worksheet: donor's name and contact information, when was the collection received and when was it accessioned, dates of the collection, condition and what preservation steps are needed, and size. Give the collection a title, write a brief biography or history of the organization, and write a brief scope and content note.

3. Preservation: Continue any minor cleaning needed, replace boxes as needed, replace only damaged folders at this time, and provide temporary labels with title and shelf location.
4. Prioritize the collection for final processing based on the local history archive's procedures. Is your queue for final processing established by order of receipt, so that each accessioned collection receives final processing one after the other? What criteria determine if a new accession moves to the front of the processing line (such as additions to previously processed collections or a collection for which users are requesting access)? What is the projected processing level for this collection?
5. Enter the information from the accession worksheet into the library's online catalog and local history archive's accession register if a separate register is used.
6. Proceed to Processing Step 4: Arrangement.

PROCESSING STEP 4: ARRANGEMENT

Your task is to *discover* the series in the collection, not to create them.

–David Carmicheal, *Organizing Archival Records*

During Processing Steps 1–3, you gathered information about the contents and dates of the collection, the condition and preservation needs of the various materials, and the biography or history of the collection's creator, and you prioritized the collection for processing at an appropriate level. In "Processing Step 1: Appraisal," you decided to acquire the collection for the local history archive. In "Processing Step 2: Legal Transfer," you stated the name of the donor, their contact information, and the approximate size of the collection, you identified any restrictions requested and/or required, and you gave the collection a temporary or perhaps permanent name. Also, in Step 2, you gained legal transfer of the collection. During "Processing Step 3: Accessioning," you gave the collection an accession number and a collection number to track its receipt and to uniquely identify it among all other collections. You created MARC records in the library's online catalog from all the information you entered onto the accession worksheet. In some collections, the original order and the series of materials are clear; thus, their arrangement and description is seldom complicated. You may ask, what is left to do? Large collections need more arrangement, but how much arrangement and/or rearrangement is required, and why?

Most everyone who writes about archival work agrees that the basic purpose of processing is to make the collections findable, available, and useable for patrons/users. In a literature review of traditional archival theories and various manuals compared to current, twenty-first century writings, none was without a variation of this statement somewhere in their pages. Disagreed about mostly is how we achieve processing—archival appraisal, accessioning, arrangement and description, and access methods—that will make the contents of collections findable, available, and useable. Archival processing narrows the search for the information that answers users' questions.[11]

Development of policies and procedures to gain intellectual and physical control in order to maintain, preserve, and make materials available for research is critical. All collections are more valuable when fully accessible, and integrated control and finding aids create the finishing touches for researchers. The following searchable elements are necessary: name of author or creator, title, dates covered, size/number of units, donor, biographical or historical note, a scope and content note, series descriptions, and access points such as subject entries.

■ Definitions

Arrangement (SAA, 34-35): The process of organizing materials with respect to their provenance and original order, to protect their context and to achieve physical or intellectual control over the materials. The organization and sequence of items within a collection.

Arrangement (*OLDIS*): In archives, the process of putting records into order, following accepted archival principles, with special attention to their provenance and original order. If, upon careful scrutiny, the original order is found to be completely random, the archivist may, after carefully documenting the original sequence, substitute an impartial arrangement that is more convenient to use.

Arranging and creating descriptions of manuscripts and archives differs from cataloging print materials. There are no title pages, tables of contents, or indexes to aid in the description, and each group is unique in some way, even when some parts of the collection are similar in type or content to others. Whatever the material, description of manuscripts and archives serves the same purpose as cataloging and classification of print materials—to make them available for research purposes.

Levels of Arrangement and Description

Archival processing operates at five levels of arrangement and description: repository, record group or collection, series, file unit, and item. Each level is coordinated with the other. The "repository" is the local history archive. The term "record group" usually refers to records created by an organization, business, or government. The term "collection" is most often used for records created by an individual, family, or self-identified group of people. "Series" are divisions of the records or papers, such as correspondence, letters, financial files, and executive board minutes. A "file unit" simply means a file folder of records that relate to the same activity, such as letters from mother, a subject such as baseball, or a transaction such as the purchase of stocks. "Items" are the individual items within the folders (for example, a multi-page letter is most often considered one item). These levels apply to paper files and folders, as well as computer files and folders.[12]

■ Five Levels of Arrangement and Description Example ───

Repository	Repository
local history archive	local history archive
Record group	**Collection**
Jones Saddle Company Records	Rev. Tom Rivers Papers
Series	**Series**
President's correspondence	Sermons
Sub-series	**Sub-series**
Incoming correspondence	None
Outgoing correspondence	None
File Unit	**File Unit**
May 1965	1860–1870
May 1965	1871–1880
Series	**Series**
Business Office files	Photographs
Sub-series	**Sub-series**
Audit reports	None
File Unit	**File Unit**
1965	1888

■ Definitions

Record group (SAA, 330): A collection of records that share the same provenance and are of a convenient size for administration. A record group is a hierarchical division that is sometimes equivalent to provenance, representing all the records of an agency and its subordinate divisions.

Record group (*OLDIS*): In archives, an aggregation of all the records of a particular agency or person, or a body of records known to be related on the basis of provenance, usually stored together in their original order. A *record subgroup* consists of records within a record group, related in some way (functionally, chronologically, geographically, etc.) or produced by a subordinate unit of the agency responsible for creating, receiving, or accumulating the group.

Series (SAA, 358–359): Series are a group of similar records that are arranged according to a filing system and that are related as the result of being created, received, or used in the same activity.

Record series (*ODLIS*): In archives, records of the same provenance, determined upon inspection to belong together because they 1) are part of a recognizable filing system, 2) have been stored together because they were produced by the same activity, 3) are related to the same function or activity and are similar in format, or 4) comprise a set logically grouped in some other way.

The first step in arranging a collection—whether original order is evident or not—is to research the creator, organization, or agency and the activities of the person or institution. The processing archivist/librarian verifies the dates of the materials, confirms personal identifications, reviews published information about the person or organization, and begins a biographical or agency history file. This information assists in clarifying unclear series and in describing the collection.

Review the record group/collection to gain an understanding of the materials contained. Add to the knowledge gained during appraisal and accessioning, and look for subdivisions within the collection's arrangement as received from the donor. These subdivisions are the series level. Take, for example, personnel files of the sales department or Aunt Mary Jones's correspondence. In looking at each instance, do sub-series exist, do the personnel files series contain the sub-series of training files and evaluation files, and are these obvious in the original order? Aunt Mary Jones separated her correspondence by the name of the individual "Cousin Bob Jones," whose letters she received; these letters are a sub-series. Look for logical and consistent filing systems. Keep together files labeled, for example, "CEO's correspondence" and those labeled "committee files and financial records." File units are the file folders containing the records. Items are the individual letters from Cousin Bob within Aunt Mary's correspondence.

Organizational charts and filing rules help in reviewing the functions of an organization and determining original order, subgroups, and series. The records of an organization or business might arrive organized by series that follow the organizational chart of the creator, such as the Office of the President/CEO, Finance Office, Legal Department, Personnel, Board of Directors, Development/Fundraising Office, Public Affairs/Relations, IT, or Facilities. Organizations can evolve through several decades and several names before becoming the organization from which the archival records are received. For example, the Jones Saddle Company Records (the group) contain the Jones Trading Post Records (the subgroup because these are records of the predecessor business). The records (the group) might or might not contain subgroups of the predecessor agency. Within each subgroup, series relating to functions, such as administrative series, committee series, financial series, and public relations series, will appear. Within these series are subseries of correspondence, minutes, press releases, tax files, case files, special project files, etc., grouped together by the creators because of the relationships arising out of their creation, receipt, or use. The series and subseries can relate to a particular subject or function, result from the same activity, or have a common form.

Materials filed together by format such as oversized drawings, maps, or photographs, constitute series, as do oral history audio recordings kept together as a series with transcripts and/or interviewee files. Series can and do contain a variety of formats, however. Correspondence series—whether letters on paper or letters in electronic and digital files on CD-ROMs or USB drives—all belong to the correspondence series. File units are file folders, bound volumes, microfilm reels, or magnetic disk packs. Within the file units, arrangement is alphabetical by creator, chronological, geographical, subject, or even numerical order.

■ Possible Series Found in Organizational and Business Records Example

Bylaws or charter
   Chief executive officer files
Committee minutes
Convention or yearly meeting files
   Correspondence
Executive board minutes

Financial records
   Legal files
Legislative files
Membership or stockholders records
   Organizational charts
   Personnel records
Policy and procedures manuals
   Public relations files
Publications
   Special projects files

All organizations and institutions share similar types of records. A typical local history archive collects archival records from the League of Women Voters, the Rotary Club, local churches, garden clubs, the historic preservation society, lumber mills, factories, florists, morticians, newspaper publishers, and library clubs, among others. To ensure that only records of enduring value from such groups are sent to the local history archive, records schedules are established, especially when additions/accretions can be anticipated. The life cycle of a record means its existence from creation—the day the letter was written—to final disposition—the day the correspondence files were sent to the archive or the day the file was destroyed according to a records schedule. Laws govern the life cycle of some records, such as financial ones. Federal tax laws require financial records of profit and nonprofit agencies to be kept for seven years (always check current rules on the IRS website) from the date of the tax statement. After that time, financial records (such as cancelled checks and bank statements) are candidates for disposal according to records schedules. In contrast, correspondence and committee minutes are considered permanent archival records. By using records schedules, permanently valuable records can be transferred to the archive, and non-archival materials can be destroyed at the appropriate times (see an example of a retention schedule on page 46). The organization or business can designate a staff member as the records manager. Clubs and societies sometimes establish an archive or history committee to be responsible for records.

A collection created by an individual or a family does not have records schedules and seldom filing rules. Some individuals do have a filing system for their collection if it is very large, but not as often as do local business or churches. The type of record, the activity documented, or the function of activities within a manuscript group of personal papers identifies series and can include correspondence, legal and financial papers, diaries, and photographs. Are the Jones Family Papers in the Everytown Public Library Local History Archive (see Scenario A, page 21) grouped by function, such as correspondence, financial records, legal records, business files, civic activity involvement, school records, genealogical files, and land records? Within these function-related files and series, is there a chronological order or an alphabetical order? Maintaining the original order in which the collection is received also preserves context.

Items that are non-archival, such as duplicate copies of the organization's newsletter, copies of the town newspaper available elsewhere in the library, vouchers and invoices for routine office supplies more than three years old, canceled checks and bank statements more than seven years old, and duplicate reading and clipping files, can be eliminated. The local history archive does not need to keep 100 copies of the organization's various promotional brochures. Two copies of each are appropriate for the organization's archives. Other copies can be placed in the library vertical files and exhibitions file, if wanted. Samples of blank stationary and invoices might also be kept for an exhibitions file because of decorative letterheads.

Formats of the physical items are not unique. Every collection will contain some of the same type of functional materials (such as correspondence) and many of the same formats (such as microfilm and CDs). But based on content of the materials within archival and manuscript collections, the items are unique. Within a collection, photocopies of original correspondence can exist. The original correspondence can also reappear in microfilm and computer files such as PDFs. Arrangement procedures in the department's processing manual might instruct you to keep only the original correspondence because of space limitations, to keep all copies in every format as part of the collection, or to eliminate multiple photocopies and keep only microfilm and PDFs. For example, John Jones's grandfather's original letters to his wife, 1800 to 1852, contain unique information. Photocopies contain the same information in a different format, but they are not the original archival letters. Content of fragile or damaged letters kept in a different format is extremely helpful when users wish to review the letters. Once an arrangement of the collection is discerned, materials can be rehoused into archival folders and boxes, and other appropriate containers. The processing procedures manual for appraisal, accessioning, arrangement, and description of archival materials—updated consistently and as needed—is always followed.

Although, "arrangement" is listed as Step 4 of processing and "description" as Step 5, these two steps occur at the same time for consistency and efficiency. In "Processing Step 1: Appraising" and "Processing Step 3: Accessioning," what have you learned about the arrangement of the collection? What decisions have you made about how to proceed? You have given the collection a title, determined the dates of the collection, written brief biographies and/or organizational histories, and drafted a scope and content note explaining what the collection is about and what materials it contains. As you review the arrangement of the collection do your decisions still hold true, or do you, for example, need to broaden the scope and content notes and expand the dates?

Does the original order exist and what groupings of materials by type of document, function of items, or format of files are in the collection? Your answer to this last question might actually be a list of series in the collection, such as correspondence arranged alphabetically by sender (type of document), financial records arranged chronologically (function of items), and oversized architectural drawings (format of materials). Identifying the series maintains the original order and most likely leads you to the final arrangement. If you are still unsure of the series in the collection because some materials such as correspondence appear in different formats (for example, original letters, 1900–1980, and an electronic file of correspondence, 1981–2000, plus some correspondence is financial not personal correspondence), then instead of physically moving materials around like jigsaw puzzle pieces, compose lists of materials so that the series reveal themselves. Intellectual rearrangement takes less time than physical rearrangement, especially with large collections and with small collections for which original order has been lost.

■ Examples of Arrangements

Example A: Jones Saddle Company–original arrangement

Box 1

  Folders 1-6 John Jones letters, 1960-1980
  Folders 7-10 Business office files, 1960-1980
  Folder 11 Treasurer's correspondence 1960-1970

Box 2

  Folders 1-14 Business office files, 1981-2000
  Computer external hard drive 1, John Jones letters, 1981-1991
  Folders 15-20 Treasurer's correspondence, 1971-1980

Example A: Jones Saddle Company–description

  Series 1–John Jones's letters, 1960-2000
  Series 2–Business office files, 1960-2000
  Series 3–Treasurer's correspondence, 1960-2000

Arrangement: If the collection consists of a few boxes or a few stacks of files it should take minimal time to physically arrange them by Series 1, Series 2, and Series 3. Add short series descriptions: Jones Saddle Company, Series 1, John Jones's letters, 1960–2000, contains correspondence among Jones as president of the company, customers, and other company employees.

Example B. Jones Saddle Company–original arrangement

Box 1

  Folders 1–4 Business office files, 1960–1980
  Folders 5–19 Business office files, 1981–2000

Box 2

  Folders 1–7 Treasurer's correspondence 1960–1980

Box 3

  Folders 1–6 John Jones letters, 1960–1980
  Computer external hard drive 1, John Jones letters, 1981–2000

Box 1 is Series 1, Business office files, 1960–2000
Box 2 is Series 2, Treasurer's correspondence, 1960–2000
Box 3 is Series 3 John Jones's letters, 1960–2000.

No physical rearrangement is necessary and the description will include series descriptions such as Series 3, CEO Correspondence, 1960–1980, John Jones's letters contains correspondence among Jones as president of the company, customers, and other company employees.

Example C. Jones Saddle Company original arrangement

Box 1 1960–1980

  John Jones letters
    Folder 1 1960
    Folder 2 1961

  Business office files
    Folder 3 1960
    Folder 4 1961

  Treasurer's correspondence
    Folder 5 1960
    Folder 6 1961

Box 2 1981–2000

  John Jones letters
    Hard drive 1, 1981–2000

  Business office files
    Folder 1 1981
    Folder 2 1982

  Treasurer's correspondence
    Folder 3 1981
    Folder 4 1982

Box 1 contains folders from Series 1, Series 2, and Series 3, as does Box 2. Should these folders be physically rearranged? *NO.* The company kept their filing system in chronological order each year, and it should remain this way. The series description should, however, describe what is contained in Series 1: John Jones's letters, 1960-2000, contains correspondence among Jones as president of the company, customers, and other company employees.

How can a user access one series from such an arrangement of records? How does the reference staff find them? The description within the finding aid leads to the files the users want to review. For a researcher to review all of the Business Office files, both Box 1 and Box 2 will need to be accessed by the user. If a user is interested only in the 1964 files of the business office, only Box 1 will need to be accessed. Folder numbering begins over again from 1 within each box. This is not always necessary within a small collection, but it is extremely helpful for collections with more than three boxes up to a thousand boxes.

Within archival arrangement at the group/collection, series, folder, and item level, physical activities vary based upon the department's processing plan and arrangement and description procedures. A newly established local history archive might develop plans and procedures for processing all accessions equally. For example, the Jones Saddle Company Records arrive in an original order of two subgroups: the Jones Trading Post Records, and the Jones Saddle Company Records. Identified series are: 1) John Jones CEO letters, 2) business office files, and 3) Treasurer's correspondence. The file level is chronological: John Jones Letters, 1960–1980, folders 1–6, etc. Each box and folder is examined to verify that its contents are placed in this order and that items within folders are in chronological order; for example, Box 3, Folder 1, John Jones Letters, 1960, January 1–January 31. Some organizations file records in reverse chronological order; for example, Box 3, Folder 1, John Jones Letters, 1980, December 31–December 1. This original order is maintained. All boxes and all folders will be replaced with archival boxes and folders.

Needed routine preservation activities are also completed at this stage. Traditional processing preservation activities include removing metal clips and staples, interleaving or photocopying highly acidic items (such as newspaper clippings), and unfolding oversized items and removing them to appropriately sized boxes and folders. (See Chapter 4 for more information on preservation.) Description is thorough with a broad scope and content note, an extensive biographical note, series descriptions, a container list, and multiple subject access points. The time it takes for a librarian/archivist to arrange and describe one linear foot of archives and manuscripts as described here is estimated to be 15 hours. This is an average estimate that combines processing times for collections already in very good physical order and needing very few preservation activities with collections in poor physical order and needing extensive preservation activities. The processing experience of the archivist and the non-processing responsibilities of the archivist might or might not be included in the calculations. Each local history archive is required to balance processing time against all other departmental responsibilities and the abundance or lack of resources.

Librarians/archivists develop thoughtful, professional plans and procedures for processing accessions on a sliding scale among and within collections. Collections from the earliest period of the local area (perhaps the early nineteenth century) will be prioritized for high processing, or these levels could be stated as Priority 1 processing (meaning traditional archival processing). Such a collection (for example, the Rev. Tom Rivers Papers, 1860–1890, small and in fair physical condition) is a good candidate for the digital reformatting and an Internet access program. This work will require approximately 15 hours per foot to process and digitize the Rev. Rivers Papers, or a total of 52.5 hours (6 and ¾ work days) for 3.5 linear feet. Large, twenty-first century collections sometimes, depending on content, are prioritized for low processing (Priority 3 processing), which means streamlined or minimal arrangement and description. Such a collection (for example, the Jones Saddle Company Records, 1960–2000) consists of 100 linear feet of files in original order. The condition of the records will vary from fair to very good, and a mixture of formats, from computer discs to videotapes, can be contained. Low processing limits the amount of time spent on refoldering, checking order within folders, unfolding and/or removing oversize materials and rehousing them in size appropriate containers, removing metal fasteners, and photocopying acidic items. Description of the records will also be minimal, with limited amounts of access/subject points added to the inventory; series descriptions are optional. This type of processing is estimated to require only about four hours per linear foot, 400 hours for 100 linear feet (50 work days). Medium processing (Priority 2 processing) plans fall between high processing (the Rev. Rivers Papers) and low processing (the Jones Saddle Company Records), and processing time could vary from four to 15 hours per linear foot. The older files from the nineteenth century in the collection might receive high processing, while the newest files from 2001–2010 might receive low streamlined processing. Sampling and reviewing, for example, 20 percent of the files is appropriate for extensive files, such as 50 years of mass mailings, with the sample being only one percent of each year's mass mailing files. Preservation activities still depend on the condition of items, of course, and description of fragile items will be more traditional than streamlined. Many factors influence the decisions made by the archivist/librarian as to the assignment of processing plans: high, medium or low. Resources are the primary factor. Outside influences, such as a grant for digitization of a collection, can influence processing ranking for some collections. Another factor is the receipt of an addition to a collection that is heavily used each year. Still, the watchword is balance, and the outcome must always be access for users.[13]

Arrangement and description appear difficult to achieve, but they are not. Place the records/files into a logical order, and describe the contents. Shelve collections in a system that permits efficient retrieval. Follow the processing plan, and avoid being sidetracked by one collection to the determent of others. Small, well-ordered collections can be processed quickly, but do not avoid large collections, as this leads to a processing backlog (the processing black hole). Avoid biased processing where collections containing the processing archivist/librarian's favorite subjects or people are processed first rather than based on the processing priority. Keep moving and adding to the work already completed.

Recap: Arrangement, How to Do It

1. Review the appraisal files and notes made about the collection during appraisal and accessioning. What is the title assigned to the collection? Is an original order evident in the collection?

2. If an original order is apparent, what is it? Describe the original order, such as six boxes of correspondence from the President's office dated by year and month, and divided and labeled as incoming correspondence and outgoing correspondence. Or, three file folders of sermons written by Rev. Tom Rivers, arranged in chronological order. The President's correspondence is a series within the records (the group) of the Jones Saddle Company Records. The sermons of Rev. Rivers are a series within the Rev. Tom Rivers Papers (the group/collection). If no original order is apparent, determine if this is because file folders have lost their labels or the items have been separated from identifying folders. Sort unlabeled files and items by the person who, or the office that, created or compiled them (such as the president of the company) or by activity or function (such as sermons). The president's correspondence is a series, and the sermons are a series.

3. Compile notes about the series including size, dates, and a brief description.

4. Follow the collection's processing plan for "Processing Step 4: Arrangement Processing," and revise if needed. If your arrangement plan includes refoldering all files and removing all staples and paper clips, those steps should be completed now. Once refoldered (or not), move all files into archival boxes. Some of this work might have already occurred during appraisal and/or accessioning because of the physical condition of folders and boxes.

5. Proceed to Processing Step 5: Description.

PROCESSING STEP 5: DESCRIPTION

Description's two objectives are to provide administrative control for the repository and establish intellectual control for staff and users through finding aids and descriptive access created by the local history archive. Indeed, the ultimate purpose of arrangement and description is connecting users to collections.

■ Definitions

Description (SAA, 112): The process of creating a finding aid or other access tools that allow individuals to browse a surrogate of the collection to facilitate access and that improve security by creating a record of the collection and by minimizing the amount of handling of the original materials.

Archival description (*OLDIS*): A general term encompassing both the cataloging of archival and manuscript collections and the production of finding aids (inventories, registers, indexes, and guides) to assist users in accessing such materials.

Description of archival and manuscript collections builds on the previous processing steps and the processing plan for each collection. You'll discover by the time you reach "Processing Step 5: Description" that some collections are completely processed except for finishing touches on the finding aids. For example, the Rev. Tom Rivers Papers has an accession record that serves as the collection's entry in the library's online catalog (the ILS). The only two actions remaining are to fill in any blanks in the descriptive elements, scope and content notes, biography, and series descriptions, and to add additional access points/subject entries to the record if needed. (See the example inventory for the Rev. Tom Rivers Papers in the Recap Description section on page 94.)

During the review of a collection's physical condition, make notes and references to the contents of the materials. Date, creator, and/or recipient identify correspondence and other series. The hoped-for outcome are descriptive roadmaps to the contents of collections for the purpose of user access. The resulting descriptions fall into several categories: online catalog entries, guides, finding aids, registers, or inventories. As the processor continues to prepare the description, she will look for items in need of repairs or special treatment.

Just as a roadmap is seldom designed to provide a description of each town, or even state, through which the mapped roads traverse, an archival descriptive roadmap does not stop to provide a description of each document or item within the collection. Nor does the processor give an in-depth historical setting or background for each item. The descriptions should be clear, concise, and consistent at each level, and written free of jargon and arcane terms. Do not overly concentrate on one series. Collections are described at the series level—not item by item—while retaining the context among the items within the collection. Item level description is not cost effective for a local history archive that is actively collecting. Exceptions, however, can be necessary for autograph collections, literary collections in which each item has a high monetary value, non-published (manuscript) maps, and collections of only a few items. For the local history archive, an item listing of a small collection of rare documents written by the namesake of the town might be item indexed because of the woman's significance to the town and region. This collection might also have been deemed appropriate for digitization during "Processing Step 1: Appraisal" and "Processing Step 3: Accessioning." The needed metadata, names, dates, creator, etc., is already gathered for many items and can be completed during description.

■ Definitions

Metadata (SAA, 248): A characterization or description documenting the identification, management, nature, use, or location of information resources (data).

Metadata (*OLDIS*): Structured information describing information resources/objects for a variety of purposes.

Finding Aids

How the collection is arranged and described will determine if, and how quickly, the user can find answers. Utilize specific local knowledge to write inventories that make it easier for users to efficiently find answers and avoid reading lengthy descriptions of collections irrelevant to their questions. Adopt and follow consistent policies for describing collections. The accession record serves as the first finding aid created for a collection; this is the beginning of a unified descriptive system. The accession finding aid gives the location of the collection in the local history archive, identifies the source or provenance, and outlines the general contents of the collection providing administrative control. Each next level of description builds on this information, including inventories and container lists.

Processing Steps 1–4: Appraisal, Legal Transfer, Accessioning, and Arrangement provide the information needed for preparing a descriptive inventory of the collection. All parts of an inventory should be specific to the collection being described. Typical inventories will include repository administrative information such as the local history archive's policies on access and restriction, receipt and accession dates, collection number, and a list of related collections. The next section will discuss provenance and donor information, and give an overview of the collection contents. The biography or agency history gives the principal events in the person's life or in the agency's life during the period covered by the collection. A scope and content note tells what types of materials are included, and the dates of the collection's materials (beginning and end, as well as bulk dates) where most materials are concentrated. For example, the collection might contain materials that begin with a few 1916 files and end with a few 1990 files, the beginning and ending dates, and it might contain many more files dated from 1930 to 1980, the bulk dates. The scope and content note will also name the series/important divisions of the collection and significant correspondents and subjects. The series descriptions name the series, "correspondence"; date of the series, "1930–1980"; the quantity of the series, "5 linear feet"; arrangement, "three series in chronological order"; and major correspondents and subjects, "correspondence among President Bob Jones and officers of the company, including Chief Operating Officer John Doe, Treasurer James Smith, and Vice President for Asset Allocation Jane James". If someone or something significant that a user might expect to find in the collection is missing, note this in the series description (for example, "President Jones's correspondence does not include letters from his predecessor and father, Tom Jones"). For small collections series descriptions do not repeat what is stated in the scope and content note. Access points such as subject headings direct the user to appropriate series and boxes. Finally, an inventory provides a container listing of the materials in the collection. Container lists, probably compiled during arrangement, include box numbers and box contents, and occasionally include folder numbers and contents, but not always, depending on the collection's processing plan.

■ Example Container Lists

The container listing can be brief:

SERIES President's correspondence:

FILE UNIT Box 1, 1930-1940

Box 2, 1941-1950

Box 3, 1951-1960, etc.

Or the container listing can be expansive:

SERIES President's correspondence:

Box 1, 1930-1940

SUB-SERIES: Incoming correspondence

FILE UNIT: Folder 1, Jan.–May 1930

FILE UNIT: Folder 2, June–Dec. 1930

SUB-SERIES: Outgoing correspondence

Folder 3, Jan.–May 1930

Folder 4, June–Dec. 1930 etc.

Box 2, 1941-1950

Incoming correspondence

Folder 1, Jan.–May 1941

Folder 2, June–Dec. 1941

Outgoing correspondence

Folder 3, Jan.–May 1941

Folder 4, June–Dec. 1941 etc.

Box 3, 1951-1960, etc.

Incoming correspondence

Folder 1, Jan.–May 1951

Folder 2, June–Dec. 1951

Outgoing correspondence

Folder 3, Jan.–May 1951

Folder 4, June–Dec. 1951 etc.

Descriptions of large collections can be used to overcome physical arrangement concerns. For example, during archival appraisal of the 100 archival boxes, 1922–2000, of school board records the archivist/librarian found that the creators arranged Boxes 1–30, 1922–1945, chronologically by date, and then by office of origin. For example, Box 1, Folder 1, is labeled "1922, January, Everywhere County School Board Minutes"; Box 1, Folder 2, is labeled "1922, January, Superintendent of Schools, Correspondence", etc. for all months in 1922 through December 1945. In 1946, the arrangement changes to office of origin, then chronologically by date. Box 31, Folder 1, for example, is labeled "School Board Minutes, January 1946", and it contains typed official minutes, edited drafts, and handwritten notes taken by the School Board secretary during the meetings. Box 1, Folders 2–5, are labeled "Superintendent of Schools, Correspondence, January 1946", etc. for all months in 1946 through December 1997. The records for 1998 through 2000 are in boxes wherein paper files and a number of electronic records are interfiled. Within the files for the School Board Minutes are paper copies of the official minutes and several CDs containing electronic files of the school board minutes, including the official minutes, several drafts of the minutes with editing, and handwritten notes of the School Board secretary taken during the meetings. It is not necessary to physically rearrange this large group of records—the finding aid/inventory container lists can alleviate that need.

■ Finding Aid/Inventory Container Lists Example

The Everywhere County School Board Minutes and the School Superintendent's Correspondence can be brought together intellectually through the finding aid container list for the benefit of users including the public, students, or officers and members of the School Board.

Series description: School Board Minutes, 1922-2000: This series contains original handwritten notes taken by the Secretary of the School Board during all meetings of the School Board; drafts of typed minutes with editing by other officers of the School Board; and a final, official, typed copy of the minutes. From 1922 through 1997, all files are paper. In 1998 through 2000, only the final official copy of the minutes is found in paper and the Secretary's notes and edited drafts are only found on CDs.

Series container listing:
School Board Minutes, 1922-1925

1922	Box 1, Folders 1, 6, 10, and 12
1923	Box 2, Folders 1, 7, 12
1924	Box 3, Folders 6 and 10
	Box 4, Folders 1-2
1925	Box 4, Folders 3-8

School Board Minutes, 1926–1946

1926	Box 7	
1927–1935	Boxes 9–10	
1936	Box 31	Folders 1–4
1937–1946	Boxes 46–50	

School Board Minutes, 1947–2000

1947–1962	Box 63	
1962–1985	Box 78	
1986–1997	Box 93–94	
1998–2000	Box 100	Folders 1–12, CD 1

OR

School Board Minutes, 1922–1925

Boxes 1– 4

Box 1, Folders 1, 6, 10, and 12	School Board Minutes, 1922
Box 2, Folders 1, 7, 12	School Board Minutes, 1923
Box 3, Folders 6 and 10	School Board Minutes, 1924
Box 4, Folders 1–2	School Board Minutes, 1924
Box 4, Folders 3–8	School Board Minutes, 1925

OR

School Board Minutes, 1926–1946

Boxes: 7, 9–10, 31, 46–50

School Board Minutes, 1947–2000

Boxes: 63, 78, 93–94, 100

OR

Box 1, Folders 1, 6, 10, and 12	School Board Minutes, 1922
Box 2, Folders 1, 7, 12	School Board Minutes, 1923
Box 3, Folders 6 and 10	School Board Minutes, 1924
Box 4, Folders 1–2	School Board Minutes, 1924
Box 4, Folders 3–8	School Board Minutes, 1925
Box 31, Folders 1–4	School Board Minutes, 1946
Box 100, Folders 1–12, CD 1	School Board Minutes, 2000

The argument has been made that leaving the records such as these of the school board first in chronological and then functional arrangement, rather than rearranging them into functional series, will create more work for staff in retrieving folders and boxes asked for by users. While no comparative studies on this have been done, numerous studies about archival processing times, arrangement, and description have been done. Perhaps the average processing time of experienced archivists/librarians can be lowered from the average of 15 hours per linear foot if the physical rearranging of records/ papers is minimized when possible. In some local history archives, retrieval staff time is less expensive than processing staff time, because students, rather than archivists/librarians, retrieve and reshelf materials. If the records are useable by researchers, then the original order can be maintained even when that order does not fit the traditional archival construct. Collection container lists in database software make it possible to intellectually pull together a list of boxes containing the topics/subjects files sought by users.

Standardization of finding aids benefits users and facilitates searching of materials through the Internet and through databases such as OCLC WorldCat (www.WorldCat.org). The use of common tools and standards allows the local history archive to further the goal of sharing resources, reducing costs, and providing increased access. A MARC record for each archives and manuscript collection in the public library's ILS is one of the quickest, easiest, most time-saving and cost-efficient finding aids. The proper way to enter names and subject entries is standardized and all materials entered into the public library's online catalog use the same MARC fields for each element of the bibliographic information. An entry in the ILS does not preclude the local history archive from creating other finding aids, such as inventories, and posting those on websites. "Archival description standards are the guidelines, rules, and specifications that lay down methods of producing uniform and consistent results for use in providing access to primary source materials."[14]

Utilizing all the available functions of the ILS is a money saver and a time-saver. Separate software will not need to be purchased and staff will not require training on several different software programs. Neither staff nor users are forced to search through many different interfaces. If separate archival management software or other types of proprietary or open-source software is acquired that is not compatible with the ILS, user access will be limited. Hopefully, library administrators will facilitate cooperative, time-saving, and cost-saving cataloging among library departments.

Describing Archives: A Content Standard (DACS), shows how to form the various components of a finding aid, including the collection title, names, etc., which can be correlated with, or mapped to, MARC21. Just as the Library of Congress subject headings give the standardized way to state a subject entry in MARC, DACS gives standardized ways to state a subject entry in the finding aid. DACS is an access standard used principally with library catalogs and collection inventories, the two most common access tools. Included subject entries, access points, and indexes direct users to the proper series, at least, and to the box level, at most. Much of archival description is narrative (such as the biographical/historical section of the finding aid, as well as the scope and content note, and series descriptions). The scope and content note, according to DACS section 3.1, includes the topics, events, people, and organizations to which the materials pertain. Also, subject entries are standardized. For example, you might want to add a subject access point for railroads in Montana. Based on the Library of Congress Subject Headings (LCSH), the proper MARC21 data entry would be:

650 0 #a Railroads #z Montana

"Once rendered in a consistent form and included in electronic indexes, such standardized data become a powerful tool for researchers to discover materials related to that topic." A user searching the public library's online catalog for the subject "Montana railroads," will find books, pamphlets, videos, and other published materials, as well as records for archives/manuscript collections that include information on Montana railroads because all the related MARC records contain this access point.[15]

Some local history archives provide alternative access methods such as databases, extensive subject or name indices, and lists of key subjects and dates. Create a thesaurus containing key words, subjects, terms, and names of persons and places for collections of similar content to further standardization and save time. Databases can provide broader access to photographs and other audiovisual collections, and to extensive container lists. It is helpful to note additional descriptive tools in the principal finding aid or inventory of the collection and also in the notes section of the MARC21 record. Online finding aids can contain links to these additional descriptive tools on the local history archive website. If these tools cannot be made available on the website, a designated standalone computer is required in the reference area for user access.

Archival management system software programs provide the capability to include finding aids with all access points in the library's online public access catalog (OPAC), and to publish the finding aids to the Internet with fully searchable metadata. The financial cost and staff training cost of software programs can be prohibitive to small libraries. Finding aids can, however, be economically presented on the library's website by uploading finding aids created in word-processing software that have been saved as XML (extensible markup language) documents or as PDF (portable document format) files. Inventories saved as documents in a word-processing program can be converted to PDF documents, and with the application of OCR (optical character recognition) can be web searchable. For an example, see the Grand Rapids Public Library (www.grpl.org) OPAC record for Loretta Ortt and follow the link to the PDF Inventory (http://grplpedia.grpl.org/wiki/images/d/da/003 .pdf). On the Loretta Ortt Inventory title page is information about the creation of the inventory: "This finding aid was produced using the Archivists' Toolkit, September 03, 2013, 'Describing Archives: A Content Standard' DACS."

Another way to improve search capability for finding aids is to apply Encoded Archival Description (EAD), a data structure standard that follows syntactic rules of SGML (standard generalized markup language) and XML (extensible markup language), both of which are used for programming data. EAD's "inherently hierarchical approach to data structuring mirrors the information hierarchies that have long been the cornerstone of archival descriptive practices." EAD permits finding aids to be searchable and broadly disseminated and is used to encode, or mark up, existing finding aids and to create new ones. Style sheets and macros are helpful in converting finding aids from Microsoft Word or Excel software to EAD XML files. Once converted, the files are uploaded to a web server or loaded into an XML database publishing system. Software such as The Archives ToolKit makes it possible for finding aids to be converted within the software to an Internet publishable EAD finding aid. EAD finding aids allow a repository to offer finding aids online, provide a search interface, provide online public access to a catalog record (MARC) that links to finding aids, and, within a finding aid, link digitized content of collections. The objective is to preserve access to the digital finding aid by assigning a persistent ID, the Uniform Resource Identifier (URL), which is available through the library's online catalog. Staff will need training to learn how to create EADs. New software might be required, and local history archive processing procedures will need some modification. Departments can ensure consistency in their web-based finding aids by providing processing staff with written procedures, templates, and documentation that are reviewed regularly for changes and updates.[16]

For example, for the subject entry "Montana railroads" in an EAD finding aid, the resulting encoding (the XML tags around the subject entry) would be:

```
<controlaccess>
<subject source= "lsch">Railroads- -Montana</subject>
</controlaccess>
```

As another example, an item about me might be encoded as <persname normal = "Phillips, Virginia Faye"source = "local">Virginia Faye Phillips</persname>. The tag tells any search system that my name should be handled as Phillips, Virginia Faye, but display systems will show it as Virginia Faye Phillips. The tag also tells the system that this is a locally generated name, not one from LCSH or some other naming authority.[17]

In many libraries, cataloging librarians or technical services librarians enter MARC records from finding aids created by processing librarians/archivists, as well as EAD finding aids, onto the website. Local history archives often share the services of the IT staff as well as the cataloging staff. Each public library has rules and regulations relating to the type of information placed on the library's website and the web pages of its departments. An archival management system such as the Archives ToolKit is open-source software, downloadable for free, but free software is seldom truly free. Approval to download external software programs requires authorization by the parent library and the software must meet the standards and requirements of the library's IT department. The IT and local history archive staff time required to utilize open-source software is expensive and not all public libraries can afford it.

Even if the library does not have the resources to acquire an archival management system nor staff to apply EAD, standards for titles, names, subjects, etc. are still required for access. A multiple number of finding aids, several of which use the index term *cars*, and several others which use the index term *automobiles*, or *John Jones CEO* in some cases and *Jones, John, CEO* in others, are confusing and misleading to users. Standardization limits extra staff work as well. Using archival standards is beneficial to the local history archive and its users.

The Free Library of Philadelphia rates completion of processing steps by the level/quality of access created for users to individual collections. For example, when a *"Researcher has excellent access to collection*: There is a good online finding aid (in EAD, HTLM, PDF, or other format) and there is a collection-level MARC record for the collection in the institution's OPAC and/ or in a national bibliographic utility such as OCLC. The collection may also be described in other online or offline sources that are available to researchers (such as a printed or online guide to collections)." Local history archives should strive to reach this excellent level of access. For example, search the Free Library of Philadelphia library (www.freelibrary.org) catalog for access to the name Katherine Milhous and click on the link for the finding aid. (For information on training, see this book's Conclusion and this chapter's endnotes.)[18]

Digitization

A local history archive is not required to provide digital images of all the collections it holds, nor even parts of all the collections. However, there are many valid reasons for digitizing archives and manuscripts. Digitization of materials creates another avenue of access for users. Users, and many donors, expect that the department will have a planned digitization program, just as they expect it will have planned outreach and preservation programs. From the first appraisal review of a collection through all the processing steps, plan for potential digitization of materials. Which materials should and can be digitized and presented on the web? Consider materials in constant demand by users, such as the sermons of Rev. Rivers. Single items that are fragile (for example, the 1836 customer list of the Jones Trading Post) are also good candidates for digitization. Oversized documents and those in other difficult formats, such as the architectural drawings of the old theater renovation, should also be considered for digitization, as well as files relating to popular topics, such as genealogy charts for the Rivers Family. Consider also digitizing material for new topics that you might want to promote, such as photographs of girls' and women's sports leagues. (See Chapter 4 for digitization planning, procedures, and technical standards.)

Do not fall into the common digitization error, however, of becoming an item indexer. Creating digital images for the website is not useful without information on the appraisal, arrangement and description, and context of items chosen for digitization within the larger collection. Too often this system process has become an addictive—some would say, fun— activity rather than a tool to access collections, and it often uses large portions of the local history archive's financial and staff resources, to the detriment of all other processing and access steps. Digitization of single items and creating extensive metadata for those single items has brought us back full circle to the item indexing preferred by historians in the early twentieth century. This is not sustainable if users are to be provided access to all the collections in the local history archive. Item indexing—digitization of single items out of context—actually creates more hidden collections, rather than bringing them out of hiding.[19]

Fortunately, on November 17, 2016, the Digital Public Library of America (DPLA) Archival Description Working Group released its whitepaper "Aggregating and Representing Collections in the Digital Public Library of America" (http://bit.ly/dplaCollections). The incorporation of aggregate-level records into the Digital Public Library of America, and by extension into state and local digital libraries, is recommended. Following traditional archival descriptive practices, aggregate-level metadata describes not the individually scanned items in the grouping; instead, it describes the group. As an example, consider a folder of correspondence dated 1960–1961 in the Jones Saddle Company President's records that is arranged and described as a part of the President's Correspondence Series. After each individual letter is scanned, the resulting metadata that is created is for the folder labeled, "1960–1961 correspondence". Each scanned item is represented by the aggregate-level metadata, even though each digital object/item has an individual URI (Uniform Resource Identifier) that is persistent, a PURL. The Archival Description Working Group states that the "key distinction between item-level and aggregated objects is related to descriptions of aggregations of objects: either as a sequence of individual items or as a single aggregation of items." Digital projects that create metadata more closely aligned with archival hierarchical context will improve user access.[20]

Planning is affected by the library's commitment to a digital program. Many librarians/archivists feel "tension between the move toward less processing and more description at the series level and the need for item-level cataloging and metadata for digital access." Digitization programs will, of course, vary by institution but digital standards are necessary for wider user access. Dublin Core is a standard metadata schema for digital objects, just as MARC and EAD are standards for structuring descriptive metadata about collections. It is critical to plan for the amount of metadata normally collected for each collection's items being digitized. While digital object manager software systems (such as OCLC's ContentDM and Islandora from LYRASIS Digital) present a unique identifier for each digital object, metadata can be applied to groups of images with aggregate metadata.

Metadata serves several functions. *Administrative metadata*, for example, contain the accession record date and source of acquisition and information on any restrictions. *Descriptive metadata* comes from the collection's descriptive inventory sections, and it includes the content and form of the materials. *Preservation metadata* is contained in the processing plan for reformatting and repairing materials. In an archive collection, similar items will have common metadata that can be repurposed. For example, a series of correspondence from one person in a collection may likely include the same correspondents and similar dates of another person's correspondence in the collection. Metadata can be duplicated for each item with the necessary changes to reflect the uniqueness and create the URI of each object. A photographer's collection series, "Portland street scenes for 1940", will have common metadata even though each image is unique. "The goal is to maximize descriptive metadata collection while minimizing the amount of additional descriptive and item-level work."[21]

Unknown Provenance

If during an assessment/survey of collections a variety of materials for which provenance is unknown are found, the established processing steps should be followed the same as if these materials were part of a new accession. Appraise these collections and materials. For example, if they fit the collecting focus, look for evidence of the possible donors in library records, determine the physical condition of the items, and go through all the questions normally asked about a new accession. If the decision is to keep these collections and materials, proceed with the next processing steps. If a common personal, family, or organization name is not evident, then determine if collections can be made by common characteristics, formats (such as photographs), the subject (such as local churches), or a theme (such as volunteer organizations). If possible, avoid using the title "miscellaneous." Arrange and describe these collection materials by following the established practices. It might be impossible to have a legal transfer of the materials, so document any background information you can find about the materials. "In the course of their regular activities, individuals, archival repositories, and other institutions may also consciously acquire and assemble records that do not share a common provenance or original but that reflect some common characteristic, such as a particular subject, theme, or form. Such collections are part of the holdings in most institutions and must be described in a way that is consistent with the rest of the holdings."[22]

The next and final processing step is providing users access to completed collections through multiple platforms and outreach.

Recap: Description, How to Do It

1. Review the following collection inventory for the Rev. Tom Rivers Papers. The information contained is derived from the work done in Processing Steps 1–4. At the end of Step 5, any necessary additional descriptive information is added to complete the inventory.

Example Inventory/Finding Aid

- Rev. Tom Rivers Papers, 1860–1890
- Accession number: 8–10–92/009
- Date of receipt/accessioned: 8–10–92
- Collection number: MSS 234
- Title of collection: Reverend Tom Rivers Papers
- Dates of collection: 1860–1890
- Size of collection: 3.5 lf

- Provenance: Name and address of source/donor: Donation of the Rivers Family, Everytown, State, in 1960.
- Restrictions/terms governing use: None
- Arrangement/organization: Arranged in three series, Sermons 1860–1868, 2.5 lf, Box 1; Photographs 1860–1890, 40 items, .05 lf, Box 2; and Scrapbook 1880–1890, 1 item, .05 lf, Box 3.

Biographical/historical note: Tom Rivers (1834–1891), the son of John (1801–1870) and Susan Gray Rivers (1804–1867), was born in Savannah, Georgia and migrated with his family to Everytown, State, in 1840. Tom and his six brothers and sisters attended a school established by their parents on the Rivers Ranch, where he completed the 6th grade. From 1846–1850 Tom attended the Next Town Boarding School and after graduation attended the State Baptist Seminary in Sparksville. He served as a minister in several small towns until appointed Reverend of the Everytown Baptist Church in 1856. In 1857, he married Rebecca Stone (1840–1895) from Next Town and they had five children. Their oldest son, Tom Rivers Jr., began Rivers Railroad Supplies Company in 1876. Rev. Tom and Rebecca Rivers are buried in the Everytown Baptist Church Cemetery, as are a number of their children and grandchildren.

Scope and content note: The papers relate to Rev. Tom Rivers and his life as a Baptist Minister arranged in three series. In the scrapbook, family items and mementoes are included. The photographs are mostly cabinet cards but some other types of photographs are included. The photographs are a mixture of family-, church- and town-related images.

Series Descriptions

Box 1   Sermons 1860–1868, 2.5 lf.
Box 2   Photographs 1860–1890, 40 items, .05 lf.
Box 3   Scrapbook 1880–1890, 1 item, .05 lf.

Access Points

Subject added entry—topical term: sermons
Subject added entry—topical term: photo prints
Subject added entry—topical term: scrapbooks
Subject added entry—geographical: Sparksville, State
Personal name as added entry: Rivers, Rebecca Stone (1840–1895)
Corporate name as added entry: Rivers Railroad Supplies Company
Corporate name as subject: Everytown Baptist Church,
        Everytown, State
Personal name: Rivers, Tom (1834–1891)

Existence/location of originals: Everytown Public Library Local History
Archive
Related materials: Rivers Railroad Supplies Company Records;
Sondra Rivers Papers
Languages: English
Finding aid available: catalog record ILS, inventory.
Processing archivist/date processed: Jane Doe, March 12, 1992.
Repository: Everytown Public Library Main Branch Local History Archive,
Everytown, State.

1. Write the collection inventory based on the information you've gathered
   during Processing Steps 1–4, as shown in the example above.
2. Complete needed information for your collection inventory in Step 5.
3. Follow descriptive standards: MARC, DACS, and local processing manual.
4. Update the collection's catalog record in the ILS.
5. Follow local processing manual for standardized format for the completed inventory, printed and online.
6. Proceed to Processing Step 6: Access.

PROCESSING STEP 6: ACCESS

The final step in processing archives and manuscript collections is creating
user access to the materials contained in the local history archive. Access is
at the top of the pyramid of processing steps. All steps lead to access.

■ Definitions

Access (SAA, 2): The ability to locate relevant information through the use of catalogs,
indexes, finding aids, or other tools.

Access Policy (*OLDIS*): A formal written statement issued by the person(s) or body
responsible for managing archives or special collections, specifying which materials
are available for access and by whom, including any conditions or restrictions on use,
usually posted or distributed by some method to users.

Access Policy

The local history archive seeks to provide user access to materials and collections while respecting donor requested restrictions and legal restrictions, such as copyright and privacy. An access policy lists those who can use the materials, states any restrictions to their use, and gives information regarding access to unprocessed collections. Procedures to carry out the access policy are stated as well. An access policy might identify users as the public with research interest in local resources, and/or all students. Users are also identified in the collection development policy (see Chapter 2). Some mission statements, such as that of the Athens (GA) Regional Library System, Athens-Clarke County Library, The Heritage Room, note the collection's users:

> The Heritage Room is a special collections unit of the Athens-Clarke County Library, which collects, preserves, organizes, and makes available on a limited basis materials for the purpose of research and/or preservation covering the Athens area. A publicly accessible and non-membership genealogy and local history collection, the Heritage Room is a regional resource. The Heritage Room seeks to serve students of all ages and experience levels in their research (see www.athenslibrary.org under the Locations tab, Athens-Clarke County Library, Departments tab, Heritage Room).[23]

The access policy lists any use restrictions to the collections. For example, to view fragile materials and high-value rare items, users must make an appointment for viewing. Some collections are restricted because of copyright and privacy laws, and some segments of collections are restricted to users because of donor requirements. An access policy discusses use of uncataloged/unprocessed collections that might, for example, be considered on a case-by-case basis or be closed to users until processing is complete. Other restrictions could include, for example, that only with prior approval of the archivist/librarian can appointments be made to access-approved unprocessed collections. If exceptions are made to the access policy, reference personnel should be notified.

The access policy includes procedures for reference and in-house use. For example, will users need to fill out a registration form and show identification in order to access archives and manuscripts? Are users interviewed before or after they use local history archive materials? Are cameras and other types of equipment, such as video recorders, permitted in the research room or area? Present information on handling archives and manuscript collections to users and make accommodations for access to all formats of the materials. Security of materials requires a user area separate from the public areas of the library—hopefully, a separate research room. When space is minimal, place tables with signs reading "local history archive users only" where staff can see researchers and the materials being used. If appointments are necessary to visit or to use certain types of materials, state so on the website. When visitors complete their registration forms for viewing the collection materials, give them the rules and regulations, including the copyright information, and who to contact for permission to publish or utilize the materials in websites, etc.[24]

■ **Access Policy, Procedures, and Rules Example** ─────────────

Norfolk's Local History and Genealogy Collection's access policy and its procedures and rules are posted on the department's web page. The Sargeant Memorial Collection is Norfolk's Local History and Genealogy Collection (a part of the Slover Library), contains materials about Virginia, North Carolina, West Virginia, Washington DC, and Maryland. On the Norfolk Public Library website (www.norfolkpubliclibrary.org) click the Local History & Genealogy tab, then click the SMC Collection tab, then the Special Collections & Archives tab for the Reading Room Policy.

UTILIZING THE ONLINE PUBLIC ACCESS CATALOG

Even if there is a written and publicized access policy, users cannot ask for access if they do not know that collections relevant to their research interest exist in the local history archive. A MARC record in the public library's online catalog for each collection is imperative for the best user access. The public library has an ILS, and the online public access catalog, the OPAC, is familiar to library users. Inserting MARC records for the local history collections is as straightforward as inserting a MARC record for published materials such as books.

In 2012–2013, the Yakima Valley Libraries (www.yvl.org) in Washington State consolidated the materials from several local history archives into one central storage location. (Click on the Yakima County Heritage Digital Collection tab for example collections.) Records for the collections were entered into the various libraries' online catalogs so the materials could be located and accessed by users. The libraries in Yakima Valley worked to increase the public's awareness of the consolidated collections through public presentations, catalog entries, and by creating finding aids accessible on the Internet and actively promoting the material on institutional websites and social media sites. Publicizing and providing access to important and valuable local history collections remains a priority—and at times a challenge—for the Yakima Valley Libraries.[25]

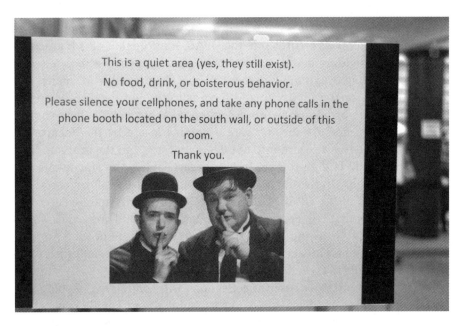

FIGURE 3.2
A friendly reminder about user rules.

Photograph Courtesy of Melissa Eastin.

Many public libraries participate in national access databases such as OCLC's WorldCat, and their MARC records from the local online catalog are searchable worldwide, 24 hours a day, every day. Thus, the MARC record for our fictional Rev. Tom Rivers Papers could be found by users from anywhere, at any time. The OCLC service ArchiveGrid pulls together over "four million records describing archival materials, bringing together information about historical documents, personal papers, family histories, and more. With over 1,000 different archival institutions represented, ArchiveGrid helps researchers looking for primary source materials held in archives, libraries, museums and historical societies." For example, the New Orleans Public Library's 237 records for local history archives and manuscript collections are included in OCLC's WorldCat and ArchiveGrid, as are the 76 local history records for the Mesa Public Library, Mesa, Arizona.[26]

If the local history archive has not entered its archives and manuscript collection records into the library's OPAC and it uses a software package for collection control and access that does not automatically connect to the ILS, check with the software company's support staff about pulling records from that software into the OPAC. For example, the current product information about PastPerfect software states that it is possible to pull a batch load of local history archive's records into the OPAC. If affordable, this is an excellent step to providing better access; however, added costs associated with the batch loading programing render this choice impossible for many. It is more efficient for the library to add records to the library's ILS whenever new collections or additions are accessioned. What are the best choices for access for users? Do the software programs in use by the department automatically enter a record into the ILS, and if not, can the program have that step added? Is the program Internet searchable? Any standalone system available only in the library can be enhanced for users by a record for each collection in the OPAC. Utilize available programs and be careful of extra programs that can create more, not less, work and cost, and usually come with a high learning curve for staff. This includes Encoded Archival Description, most archival management software programs, and such packages as PastPerfect, as well as others.

Print and archives/manuscript collections will contain overlapping subjects. For example, the East Family papers and the West Family papers both have correspondence among their forbearers as the families intermarried in the early nineteenth century. Ann East wrote letters to her cousin Sue West. Ann's original correspondence is found in the West Family Papers, while letters from Sue West to Ann East are found in the East Family Papers. Some photocopies of the correspondence are found in both collections. However, the catalog record for both the East Family and West Family manuscripts will have unique and original catalog records in the ILS. WorldCat will not have a downloadable record for the manuscripts even though a published genealogy book about the families, *East Meets West: A Family Chronicle*, written by Amber East in 1961, does have a downloadable record. Cooperation with the library's cataloging/technical services department and IT/systems department is critical in order to have all materials, including the archives and manuscript collections, about the East Family and their relatives, the West Family, accessible. The catalog librarian can create templates to handle most questions, as well as procedures to be followed for entering online records. Consistency in cataloging benefits the library and users.

Web Finding Aids

A written finding aid must be "efficient in how it presents the maximum usable information in a minimum of space and makes the essence of the collection understandable at a glance."[27] All such efficient finding aids created by the local history archive now need to be presented to users. In addition to utilizing the public library's online catalog, finding aids need to reach users in other ways, especially on websites. The best resource for learning to include finding aids is, of course, the library's IT staff who handle the proper procedures. Their procedures might require that finding aids be prepared as XML documents or PDF documents that are seachable on the Internet. Local history archives with numerous staff can assign one archivist/librarian to learn how to markup finding aids in EAD—a valuable way to create Internet searchable finding aids.

Other approaches to access might include wiki technology. In addition to a website, the Grand Rapids Public Library presents its local history finding aids in MARC format through a web page wiki, under the Research tab, and the GRPLpedia tab. The library's Loretta Ortt Papers inventory, for example, can be searched in the online catalog and through the wiki. The wiki finding aid link leads to the PDF inventory. A simple Internet search for Loretta Ortt finds the GRPLpedia PDF finding aid link. An OCLC ArchiveGrid search locates the Loretta Ortt record and includes the link to the finding aid online.

Copyright

When the public library purchases, or is given a book, only the book as physical property belongs to the library. The publishers and/or authors own the copyright of the book's contents as long as it is under copyright. It is critical to understand that a donor might legally transfer only the copyright of materials he created, and that a clear title is required. Copyright of letters written to the donor from someone else, even family members, belongs to the writer of the letters, not to the receiver of the letters. However, authors can transfer rights to the recipient of their correspondence. If joint title is held, all owners must agree to the gift or purchase. Compare this to family or group ownership of a building. One person of the group cannot sell nor transfer the ownership of the building without the written permission of all owners.

■ Definitions ───────────────────────────────

Copyright (SAA, 94-95): A property right that protects the interests of authors or other creators of works in tangible media (or the individual or organization to whom copyright has been assigned) by giving them the ability to control the reproduction, publication, adaptation, exhibition, or performance of their works. Copyright protects the owner's interests in the intellectual property (content), rather than in the physical property that serves as a container for the content.

Copyright (*ODLIS*): The exclusive legal rights granted by a government to an author, editor, compiler, composer, playwright, publisher, or distributor to publish, produce, sell, or distribute copies of a literary, musical, dramatic, artistic, or other work, within certain limitations (fair use and first sale). Copyright law also governs the right to prepare derivative works, reproduce a work or portions of it, and display or perform a work in public. Such rights may be transferred or sold to others and do not necessarily pass with ownership of the work itself. Copyright protects a work in the specific form in which it is created, not the idea, theme, or concept expressed in the work, which other writers are free to interpret in a different way. A work never copyrighted or no longer protected by copyright is said to be in the public domain.

Rights (*ODLIS*): The exclusive privilege of receiving the benefits associated with ownership of a literary property, the most important of which is the right of first publication, protected under copyright law in most countries.

Remote and in-house users require advice on how to acquire the local history archive's permission to publish, and the proper citation for quoting materials from the collection. Citation information can also be stated in collection finding aids. The library may give permission to publish materials for which the original holders have given the copyright and literary rights to the library. Users who wish to publish copyrighted materials will need owners' contact information from the library.

The conflict between users' needs and wants and copyright laws is an ever-present concern. US Copyright Act, United States Code 17, 101–1332, governs the use of published and unpublished works in the United States. The copyright law allows fair use of copyrighted materials, and permits limited photocopying or scanning of copyrighted works for use in a classroom, for a class paper or school project, or for research if such copies are not sold or given to library collections. Many collections received in the local history archive often contain photocopies of materials that donors obtained for personal research purposes, or simply for reading. Staff may retain these copies with the collections, but other patrons using the materials must obtain permission to publish from the copyright holders. For example, the Jones Family Papers in Scenario A (see pages 21–23) contain photocopies of articles from the *American Philatelist* magazine that Grandfather Jones acquired for his personal research. If another stamp collector uses the Jones Family Papers for her stamp collecting research, she may not extensively quote nor use illustrations from Mr. Jones's photocopies in a book she is writing without permission to publish from the magazine that holds the copyright, the *American Philatelist.*

Current copyright laws cover unpublished materials as well. For unpublished works, if the author is living or died less than 70 years after the date of the work's creation, the work is protected until 70 years after the death of the author. If from the date of the work's creation the author is dead and 70 years have passed, then the work is in the public domain. In the case of an unpublished work by multiple authors, it is protected until 70 years after the death of the last living author.

Anonymous manuscript works are protected for 120 years from the date of creation, or, if published, 95 years from date of first publication, or whichever term is shorter. Unpublished works that were registered with the Copyright Office (this is rare) have the same term as if they had been published (using the date of registration instead of the date of publication). The exact date a work enters, or has entered, the public domain can be determined through www.librarycopyright.net on the Copyright Genie tab. Also, visit the ALA Office for Information Technology Policy (www.ala .org) and the US Copyright Office website (www.copyright.gov/).

Employees who do work for hire, published or unpublished, do not own the copyright to the works. Their employers' own the copyright. Permission to publish from such works requires written permission from the owner organization. Government records are not covered by copyright law, nor are the works of government employees when their work is produced for the government.

Copyright restrictions and fair use law govern patron access to collections. Instructions for use of materials must make clear that copyright laws apply to any photocopies, scans, or photographs that researchers acquire. Public library local history archives might not have photocopiers and scanners available for patrons, but most users have smartphones containing cameras. Will users be allowed to photograph archival and manuscript materials? If so, users must be made aware of how copyright affects the photographs they have made of the materials. Permission to publish, including in the form of certain types of exhibitions, is still required from the copyright owner. See the copyright information on the website of the Cleveland Public Library Special Collections at http://cpl.org/thelibrary/subjectscollections/ special-collections.

Copyright law can restrict donors' wishes, too. All materials have a physical and intellectual component. Consequently, legal transfers specify what rights, other than physical, are being transferred to the local history archive. The deed of gift identifies the holder of the copyright, how long they will hold the copyright, and if the donor will transfer copyright to the library after a designated period of time. Or will heirs receive the copyright? Heirship to copyright of archives and manuscript gifts occasionally creates future problems for archivists and librarians, especially if contact information for heirs is lost. It is acceptable to ask donors to give property, copyright, and literary rights to the local history archive for the benefit of researchers and the library. Holding copyright and literary rights makes it easier for the library to grant permission to researchers to publish, create reprints of materials, or author new publications. Researchers may also seek permission for stage adaptations, movie scripts, novels, etc., and the public library can gain monetarily from royalties attached to ownership of the copyright. These generous gifts, managed properly, mean added income for the library.

The elements of legal title include physical property (the medium), and intellectual property (the message). In order for the local history archive to own a collection or item, it must have the copyright title to both the physical and the intellectual property. For example, a letter is the medium and the writing, the content, is the message. The person who received the letter is the owner of the physical property, the medium, but the sender who wrote the letter is the owner of the intellectual property, the message. Caution is needed to avoid violating the rights of either the owner of the physical property or the owner of the intellectual property.[28]

Outreach

If you build it, will they come? Yes, users researching family history, local people, and community events will find their way to you. They will also spread the word about the valuable collections in the department. Outreach is another vital component of access and local history archives must preach to users not already in their choir, including students, teachers, local community groups, preservationists, reporters, storytellers, businesses, churches, organizations and government agencies. The main purpose of outreach is to increase public awareness about the local history archive so that the numbers of users will increase. When staffs reach out to introduce programs to potential users, responses can be surprise, excitement, or wonder. An elaborate array of programs is not needed to reach out to the public and a simple plan is all that's necessary for minimally staffed departments. Exhibitions of materials can be virtual/online, but for those with appropriate space, physical exhibitions open to visitors can be combined with lectures focusing on the exhibition's contents. Participating in National Local History Day events is also public outreach and connects the local history archive with students and teachers. Also, staff members who visit schools and give speeches to organizations and club meetings expand their contacts for the department.

■ Example Outreach Programs

The Greenville County Library System South Carolina Room (www.greenvillelibrary.org, click the Learning Center tab, then the Genealogy & Local History tab) outreach efforts include a Records Search Form for remote users, and the Book-A-Librarian form to schedule one-on-one sessions with the librarian. Also, tours of the facility are followed by personalized genealogical and historical research assistance. The South Carolina Room collection includes primary and secondary sources in formats such as books, manuscripts, microforms, periodicals, databases, photographs, maps, and newspapers all searchable in the online catalog. The Grand Rapids Public Library (see www.grpl.org under the "Research" tab, Grand Rapids History & Special Collections), in addition to its variety of web pages and online digital collections, continues traditional methods of outreach such as lectures by local history specialists and workshops for users. The San Francisco History Center of the San Francisco Public Library (www.sfpl.org under Libraries tab, click Main Library for link) presents online research guides such as "How to Research a San Francisco Building." The guides lead online and in-house users to materials that are appropriate for researching buildings. The Brooklyn Public Library's Brooklyn Collection school partnership program, the Brooklyn Connections, offers workshops and school visits as well as class access to original archival materials within a standards-based project (www.bklynlibrary.org). Numerous other examples dot the websites of local history archives in public libraries.

FIGURE 3.3

"Backwards and in High Heels" Exhibit.

Courtesy of the Austin History Center, Austin Public Library. Photograph by Grace McEvoy.

What are the benefits of outreach activities, in addition to reaching new users? New users will increase usage statistics, give feedback on collection access, and provide useful suggestions on procedures and policies for other users. Users can become donors of collections and funds, and they can connect the local history archive to other potential donors and new users. This can all be used to show the library administrators and board of directors the continuing value of the department, which is, of course, important to future budgets. A well-planned outreach program should be included in the local history archive's strategic plan. Proper planning and execution lead to success.

Social media is a current, vibrant lifestyle choice for communicating. Outreach to current users, and potential new users, is also done through social media. Public libraries interact with their communities through blogs, Facebook, Twitter, Flickr, Tumblr, Instagram, wikis, YouTube, Historypin, and a variety of others. The variety changes constantly, with many new concepts introduced almost weekly. The links to social media sites on public libraries' web pages show this. The East Baton Rouge Parish Library Baton Rouge Room has recently begun to participate in web archiving by partnering "with Archive-it, an affiliate of the Internet Archive, to help collect relevant websites, social media pages and postings, videos, and blog posts" related to Baton Rouge current events (www.archive-it.org).

How does being social benefit the local history archive? Assistance for users can be posted on social media sites, and traditional outreach combined with newer social media methods will strengthen the department's community image. A blog that is regularly maintained with new information and interesting comments gets the news out about the contents of the local history archive. Comments received from the blog's readers are easy to post and share. Some departments find their blog visits constantly growing because of great public interest. Local history archives that cannot manage their own site for posting photographs from the collections can use a Flickr page. Users can post their projects and research interests in response to blogs and other sites, thereby informing staff members about subjects that need to be covered in the collections. The staff might reprioritize the processing of some collections that contain materials on subjects requested by users through social media. Announcing completed finding aids to processed collections and notes about new accessions on the sites might answer many research questions and bring new users.[29]

Public library rules can require departments to work with the public relations office that handles all traditional interactions with newspapers, radio and TV stations, as well as websites and social media. Instead of posting content on their own sites, staff submit content to the appropriate library department. The local history archive is responsible for gathering and submitting current, relevant, interesting, and useful content. If the department has its own web page, blog, and social media sites, the responsibility is the same—to provide good content that benefits the local history archive. Blogging and other social media interaction require planning, along with all other responsibilities. How much time does it take from other work, such as processing? Access achieved through processing and cataloging collections is always the first priority.

Well-considered and well-planned collection development policies, careful arrangement and description of collections, and energized access strategies are goals for all local history archives. Creating the means of access presupposes reference services.

Reference Services

We've built it, and now they will come. Reference services might be virtual or real. User questions, regardless of form, must receive prompt and professional service. Reference staff answer questions, introduce new users to finding aids, provide guidance on duplication of materials, explain copyright, direct users to further information about copyright, and interact with users in the reference room, on the phone, and online. The main objective of reference is to make the correct materials available to interested users. Users range from those knowing exactly what they wish to see when they arrive, to those who are just beginning a research project for which they have done little preparation. Users might know what they are looking for but might not know how to ask for it. Because questions can be answered in a variety of ways, staff must learn to listen carefully, and to ask more questions if the researcher's queries are unclear, in order to analyze questions and narrow a broad question down to a more precise level and determine the actual need. Users who ask for all materials on the US Civil War in the local history archive are often looking for a specific piece of information, such as a map of the area of the battle in which an ancestor died. Pointing him to the Civil War subject entry in the OPAC is not enough.

Questions range from the simplest directional questions about locating basic history texts to complex questions regarding economic development of the area. Staffing patterns for the reference desk are very important and all staff should be well trained to answer reference questions. The more staff members know about all the workings of the local history archive, the better they can answer questions. Because memory varies from day to day and personal abilities might be negatively or positively affected by conditions in a staff member's life, reference desk rotation is beneficial to both staff and users. No one staff member is required to work in reference eight hours a day, and users receive an opportunity to interact with various members of the staff. However, certain staff can be called to the reference desk to answer questions in their area of expertise when needed. Of course, large departments might have an adequate number of staff to rotate reference desk duties, and small collections might have so few staff that all must be ready to do reference at all times. Staffing assignments must match the number of staff available.

If the access policy requires users to register, a standard registration form can require them to present a valid photo ID and to sign the form before they are allowed to see materials from the closed stacks. Registration and requests for materials can be handled through computer systems rather than a number of paper forms. Registration serves three purposes: statistical, informational, and as a deterrent to theft. Statistics from registration sources show how many people are using the collection and when. Information gathered by reviewing registrations shows current research topics and when new materials relating to these topics are received. Some departments might choose not to ask users to complete a specific registration form. Some ask users to acquire a library card that serves as the access ticket to research. Others have a two-step process where the user acquires an access pass at a central information center and then presents it to the local history archive reference desk. The user produces a valid photo ID that is left at the reference desk during review of archival and manuscript materials. (Examples of user registration forms are available at the Society of Georgia Archivists Form Forum website at www.soga.org.)

If possible, the reference librarian/archivist should conduct a reference interview with each researcher embarking on a long-term project. The reference interview serves both the researcher and the staff. The researcher has an opportunity to ask detailed questions about the collection, about policies regarding photocopying, scanning, and taking photographs of materials in the collections, and other user policies. When assisting a patron beginning long-term research, the reference librarian/archivist can often point out the materials most useful to the project and ask questions that give the user an opportunity to define his or her topic. The reference interview can also lead staff to other materials appropriate for the local history archive, for users might find materials related to the research in private hands and put the staff in contact with owners. Reference exit interviews can help staff determine what areas of reference need improvement, what services the user needed but did not receive, and what compliments, and general complaints, the user has about the service or the department.

Many users will write, phone, or email before visiting in order to determine whether collections contain materials necessary to their research. Responding to user inquiries can be time consuming. All patrons deserve quality assistance; however, on-site users will probably receive priority service. A Frequently Asked Questions (FAQ) section on the website or a printed FAQ document sent to patrons is always helpful. FAQs are usually derived from the many questions asked over and over about the use of popular, unusual, or prominent collections. Maintain a file of answers to those questions so they can be reused, thereby saving staff substantial amounts of time. In some cases, non-local researchers will request an extensive review of the contents of a collection, and basically ask staff members to conduct research for them. One solution is to send these users a list of private researchers who will work under contract to do research for those who cannot visit the local history archive in person. The library might find that it necessary to implement fees for staff to answer non-local users' questions because of the amount of time needed. This should not be a problem, since users are familiar with fees for photocopies, photograph copies, and more recently, scanning.

Once the in-house user and the reference staff have identified materials specific to the user's research, materials can be retrieved. Having a system that uses call slips is a standard procedure for a user to request items and for the staff to retrieve the correct materials and leave documentation that items are legitimately removed from the stacks or storage areas. This system also improves the ability of the staff to reshelf materials properly. Computer registration and request systems consolidate many of the steps, maintain user files, and gather reference statistics. A researcher registers in the system, online or in-house, the staff verifies her photo ID, and she enters her requests for materials. Archival management system software allows her to request boxes or files directly from the online finding aid, even remotely, thus creating a shopping cart to be filled and ready for her when she arrives.

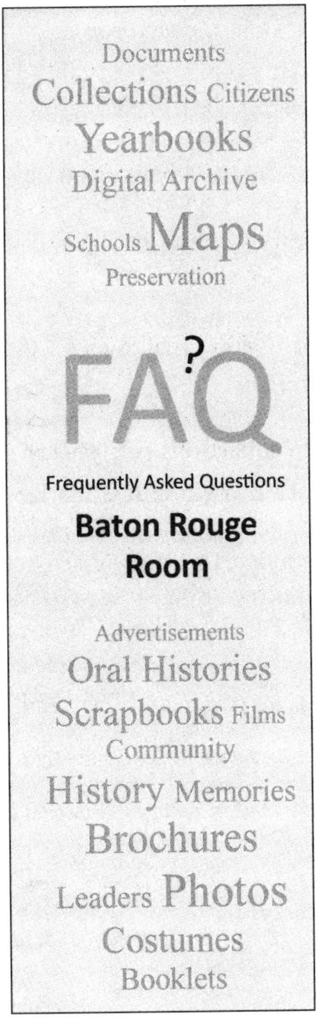

Documents
Collections Citizens
Yearbooks
Digital Archive
Schools Maps
Preservation

?
FAQ

Frequently Asked Questions
Baton Rouge Room

Advertisements
Oral Histories
Scrapbooks Films
Community
History Memories
Brochures
Leaders Photos
Costumes
Booklets

FIGURE 3.4

FAQs brochure, Baton Rouge Room.

Courtesy of the East Baton Rouge Parish Library.

After she enters her request for materials, reference staff members receive notification from the computer system, print a call slip to mark the retrieved materials space on the shelf, and deliver the requested items. When materials are returned and no longer needed by the user, the computer system allows staff to keep a record of when the materials were returned, who re-shelved them, and to add this information to the user's registration file. All steps can, of course, be done manually with paper call slips.

Patron surveys assist in understanding users needs and concerns. Questions to the patrons can cover reference, hours of operation, the scope of the collection, needs for photocopying equipment, funding, staff, or any other subject that the staff feels would benefit the department and the patrons. The resulting information can assist in providing the administration with statistics to support longer or different hours, more staffing, or other needed services.

Recap: Access, How to Do It

1. Prepare and gain administrative approval for an access policy and publicize the policy.
2. Include records for all collections in the library's online public access catalog.
3. Provide access to collections through websites.
4. Learn about copyright and how to compile with copyright laws for the benefit of the department, donors and users.
5. Develop and follow an outreach plan.
6. Through reference services guide users to the collections they seek.

Security and preservation of materials of the local history archive overlaps with, and might govern, access for the users. Both security and preservation policies include a disaster prevention and recovery policy. Chapter 4 discusses preservation, security, and disaster awareness and prevention.

NOTES

1. Richard Cox, *Managing Records as Evidence and Information* (Westport, CT: Quorum Books, 2001), xiii.
2. For the historical perspective on archival theory, read Theodore R. Schellenberg, *The Appraisal of Modern Public Records, National Archives Bulletin 8* (Washington, DC: National Archives and Records Service, 1956), and *Modern Archives: Principles and Techniques* (Chicago: University of Chicago Press, 1956).
3. Yakel, *Starting an Archives*, 31–33; SAA Glossary, 152–153, 206.
4. Cox, *Managing Records as Evidence and Information*, 24–25, 112–113, 118.
5. Ibid, 24.
6. Bastian, Sniffin-Marinoff and Webber, *Archives in Libraries*, 30, 59.

7. Society of American Archivists. Available online at www.archivists.org (Abandoned Property Project under Groups tab, Acquisitions & Appraisal Section).
8. See Standards of the Library of Congress (www.loc.gov/standards/). Developed and utilized by the Library of Congress, these are the best practices for librarians and archivists. They include authorities and vocabularies, EAD, MARC, RDA, and metadata standards.
9. Dearstyne, *Managing Historical Records Programs*, 11, 231–232; Hunter, *Developing and Maintaining Practical Archives*, 90–93, 125–127; Carmicheal, *Organizing Archival Records*, 3, 15–17, 33, 47.
10. Society of American Archivists. *Describing Archives: A Content Standard (DACS)*. Chicago: SAA, 2007. Available online at http://www2.archivists.org/groups/technical-subcommittee-on-describing-archives-a-content-standard-dacs/dacs. For a complete list of, and links to, archival standards see http://www2.archivists.org under the About Archives tab, Standards tab.
11. See for examples: Cox, *Managing Records as Evidence and Information*, 152; and Bastian, Sniffin-Marinoff and Webber, *Archives in Libraries*, 6.
12. Yakel, *Starting an Archives*, 41–43.
13. For more information on processing plans see: Hackbart-Dean and Slomba, *How to Manage Processing*, 1–5, 13–21, 35, 68–69, 135; Robert S. Cox, "Maximal Processing, or, Archivist on a Pale Horse," *Journal of Archival Organization*, 8 (2010): 134–148; and Mark Greene and Dennis Meissner, "More Product, Less Process: Revamping Traditional Archival Processing," *American Archivist* 68 (Fall/Winter 2005): 208–263.
14. This online Library of Congress publication is available at www.loc.gov under the Services tab, Library Standards tab, Resource Description Formats tab, MARC 21 formats tab.
15. SAA, *Describing Archives: A Content Standard* (DACS), xvii–xviii, 4.
16. For examples of EAD finding aids published by public libraries, see the Rocky Mountain Online Archive site of which the Pikes Peak Library District Regional History Collection is a member (www.rmoa.umn.edu and www.ppld.org). Also see: Carlsbad City Library History Collection (www.cbcl.sdp.siri.net); and the Douglas County (Colorado) History Research Center (www.douglascountyhistory.org). See also Elizabeth H. Dow, *Creating EAD-Compatible Finding Guides on Paper* (Lanham, MD: Scarecrow Press, 2005).
17. Ruth Kitchin Tillman is the EADiva (www.eadiva.com). Her website helps with understanding EAD and explains why it should be used. EADiva Tag Library is licensed under a Creative Commons Attribution 4.0 International License.
18. EAD helper files from SAA (http://listserv.loc.gov/listarch/ead.html) is an open listserv to facilitate the exchange of information about XML (Extensible Markup Language) DTD (Document Type Definition) for archival finding aids. SAA also provides the "Encoded Archival Description Tag Library," Version EAD 3, August 2015, as a free download at www.Archivisits.org/sites/all/files/taglibrary/-versionEAD3.pdf. ArchivesSpace is open source and is available through LYRASIS Digital Services at www.lyrasis.org. ArchivesSpace is used by the San Francisco Public Library, San Francisco History Center (www.sfpl.org). Innovative Interfaces commercial archives management software is used, for example, by the Tulsa City-County Library (www.tulsalibrary.org).
19. The Digital Library Federation Assessment Interest Group's working group on Cost Assessment tasks are to aggregate and make freely available a large set of data on the time it takes to perform various activities involved in the digitization process, in order to assist organizations in digitization project planning and benchmarking. The Digitization Cost Calculator, along with best practices and guidelines for the collection of time data, was created with the goal of standardizing collection of such data in the field as well as to guide data submissions to the Digitization Cost Calculator (http://dashboard.diglib.org).

20. Digital Public Library of America Archival Description Working Group, "Aggregating and Representing Collections in the Digital Public Library of America," http://bit.ly/dplaCollections, 9.
21. Hackbart-Dean and Slomba, *How to Manage Processing*, 72–74.
22. SAA *Glossary*, vii.
23. The Athens-Clarke County Library is a member of the Georgia Public Library Service PINES integrated catalog, which is powered by Evergreen open-source software, and also includes the GALILEO Library of Georgia.
24. Susan Welland, "Managing Archives in Local History Collections," in Smallwood and Williams, *Preserving Local Writers*, 156.
25. Walker, "Local Treasures," 19.
26. OCLC ArchiveGrid (http://beta.worldcat.org/archivegrid/); Athens-Clarke County Library Heritage Room (www.athenslibrary.org); and Mesa (AZ) Public Library (www.mesalibrary.org).
27. Hunter, *Developing and Maintaining Practical Archives*, 130–131.
28. Ibid, 76.
29. Emily Griffin, "Tracing History through Nontraditional Methods," in Smallwood and Williams, *Preserving Local Writers*, 324.

CHAPTER 4 | # CARE OF A LOCAL HISTORY ARCHIVE

> Archivists must anticipate and plan in order to fulfill the part of their mission that deals with preserving records of enduring value. Those records, once preserved and protected, are ready for use by researchers.
>
> **–Gregory S. Hunter, *Developing and Maintaining Practical Archives***

WHETHER THE LOCAL history archive is decades old or was formed yesterday, proper care of materials permeates every activity. Preservation, security, and disaster awareness, recovery and prevention planning should overlap everywhere. In writing the mission statement, care of the materials must be assured, for we collect and preserve to make accessible. For example, during appraisal, removing dust and dirt from paper files, and labeling boxes are all processing procedures, preservation procedures, and security procedures. Removing dust and dirt prolongs the life of the materials, thus securing them for users, and it prevents future disasters by keeping any insects that were in the dirt from being brought into storage areas. Labeling boxes, even with temporary labels, speeds arrangement and description that make materials accessible, plus it aids in securing the materials by identifying them and preventing the disaster of *lost* materials. A local history archive in a public library must work closely with other departments. Collecting and preserving materials to make them accessible requires involvement of other departments in the library's planning, including the assistance of the IT, cataloging and public relations staffs; coordination with facilities and security managers; and a designated place in disaster awareness and prevention procedures.

It is not possible in one manual to include complete in-depth preservation techniques for every type and format of material found in the local history archive. Nor is it possible to provide all the technical aspects of digitization and programing, the mechanics and procedures for security and environmental systems, nor how to write disaster prevention and recovery plans. What can be included are the broad steps necessary in all areas and suggestions on how to proceed. Understand that implementation steps in all three areas occur simultaneously and overlap continuously. Becoming an integral part of the library's planning groups and working closely with other departments will make completing seemingly daunting local history archive tasks achievable.

Numerous books, technical leaflets and articles, and how-to-do-it manuals, as well as training programs, are available to teach the step-by-step procedures for preservation, digitization, security and environmental controls, and disaster planning. The Library of Congress Preservation Division (www.loc.gov/preservation) provides free, extensive guidelines on these individual topics to all libraries. The Northeast Document Conservation Center presents free, excellent preservation leaflets on its website (www.nedcc.org). While the pamphlets are a continuing project of NEDCC, be aware that not all web links listed in the pamphlets are up-to-date. Always search by the name of the organization for current websites. The Council on Library and Information Resources' publications tab lists over 160 CLIR Reports, the most recent being published in 2016 (www.clir.org). The OCLC website (www.oclc.org) also provides numerous research publications with detailed guidance for preservation, especially for digital collections. Take some time now and review the Library of Congress Preservation Section guidelines, the NEDCC list of informational pamphlets, the CLIR Reports, and the OCLC Research Reports, and return to these as needed.

What is the most relevant preservation information and guidance needed for local history archive staffs within a public library? What roles do department librarians/archivists need to play and what responsibilities should they assume? For example, staffs need to identify collections for digital projects and outline what the local history archive hopes to accomplish with such projects. An in-house mini-preservation lab to accomplish work beyond the basics is helpful. Consider establishing quarterly preservation review sessions for staff and volunteers and discuss needs and problems at regular staff meetings. Every yearly collection assessment includes preservation, security, and disaster prevention reviews, but ongoing assessments are needed daily. Stay aware, stop when you begin to plug one more item into the power strip and ask yourself, "Is this overloaded and a fire hazard?" All staff members must be included in developing department-specific security protocols, and for disaster prevention and recovery procedures.

Local history archives, even new or young ones, might have a backlog of materials gathered by the public library in past years that needs to be reviewed for evidence of preservation issues. Attempt to sort the backlog of materials into collections. For example, if someone named Bonaventure left papers at the library, including letters addressed to several people also with the surname Bonaventure, could these papers be grouped as the Bonaventure Family papers? If no coalescing name is found, create groups by format, such as photographs or maps. Begin to tackle the backlog with appraisal steps used for new collections. During the appraisal, note any physical conditions that need to be addressed and decide if the department is equipped to handle those needs. If not, the materials must be discarded or given to another library. If the appraisal warrants keeping the materials, accession them as a named collection, such as Bonaventure Family Papers, or Everywhere County Photograph Collection, or State Maps Collection. During appraisal and accessioning, preservation concerns are noted and basic steps are taken such as transferring materials to appropriate-sized archival containers and removal of rubber bands.

PRESERVATION

Preservation, like processing, is a major program function. Usually, the preservation program takes stabilizing actions to protect the entire holdings instead of concentrating resources for item-level treatment. This approach "includes understanding the nature of the preservation problem; conducting preservation surveys to establish priorities, controlling the storage environment, planning for disasters, performing holdings maintenance, and treating selected materials."[1] These activities are appropriate for all materials, including those born digital, electronic records, audio-visual (photographs, tapes, film) and of course, paper-based materials.

Activities and procedures that ensure the long-term preservation of collections in order to make them accessible to users can be as simple as removing dust from papers or placing loose papers into folders. Other preservation steps can be extremely complex, such as identifying parts of collections to be digitized so that users can view the materials in the digital format rather than handle fragile or rare items. Preservation steps begin when materials are being reviewed for acquisition, as archival appraisal requires a review of their physical condition, as discussed in Processing Step 1: Appraisal. During appraisal, it might be necessary to remove dust and dirt, discard rubber bands, and unfold papers before being able to understand the content and make decisions about acquisition. Materials such as electronic records and audiovisual materials that require specific hardware and software are identified and evaluated based in part on the cost of making them accessible. As the appraisal proceeds and the collection is found appropriate to acquire, more preservation steps will occur, including moving materials into archival containers and removing items too damaged to save, or those whose condition is harming other materials in the collection. Processing Step 3: Accessioning, requires a second review of the condition of the collection and the preservation steps required. Further cleaning and unfolding of items might be done at this point. Segregation of the collection is mandatory when living insects are found, and elimination processes must be scheduled. During accessioning, the processing plan and the preservation plan for the collection are outlined. Assess the needs and indicate what activities are to be completed. The next review of the physical condition and preservation needs of the collection occurs during Processing Step 4: Arranging, and includes activities such as placing the collection into archival boxes and folders as needed; removing potentially damaging items such as rusting metal fasteners, rubber bands, sticky notes, plastic sleeves, etc.; and scheduling a review of audio-visual and electronic records. To fully describe (Processing Step 5: Description), the content of audio-visual materials and electronic records, a physical review through appropriate hardware and software, and probably the assistance of the IT department, is necessary to continue making decisions about how to make these materials accessible. Finding aids must identify with consistent descriptions all formats of materials contained in the collection. Digital correspondence files are noted in the correspondence series description and electronic financial spreadsheets are described in the financial records series description, even though the access to them is through the website or a standalone computer in the reference area. The basics of preservation occur at every part of collection management and extend into daily collection maintenance.

Preservation and access of materials are the goals of all activities. Policies and procedures established for proper holdings maintenance, storage, care, and handling during processing and by users, ensure both goals are met. Local history archive materials require special housing and handling for their continued availability. The physical space of the department is designed to facilitate the administration of the archival program, use of materials, preservation activities, security procedures implementation, and disaster prevention and recovery planning. Space is required for staff work areas, storage areas as the collection grows, and research and reference services. Current research on these topics changes rapidly and local history archive staff must stay aware. Create checklists to follow and review preservation, security, and disaster preparedness and recovery procedures. Examples of checklists to adapt as needed are at the end of each section in this chapter.

Reference services staff members oversee the proper care and handling of materials by public users. When users arrive, they will be introduced to the procedures to follow while handling archives and manuscripts. In addition to posting these procedures and policies on the local history archive's website, give users a printed copy. These reading room procedures and policies could include, among other instructions, steps listed in the Norfolk Local History and Genealogy Collection guidelines.

■ Policies and Programs Example

Refer back to the reading room policy of the Norfolk County Public Library's Sargeant Memorial Collection (SMC), Norfolk's Local History and Genealogy Collection, on page 98 and online at www.norfolkpubliclibrary.org. Add other rules and procedures as necessary and appropriate. Other examples of user procedures and policies are found on the websites of: the Austin History Center, Austin Public Library (http://library.austintexas.gov/ahc/visit-us); the Boston Public Library, Special Collections (www.bpl.org/research/special/); the Archives@Queens Library, Long Island Division (www.queenslibrary.org); and the San Francisco History Center of the San Francisco Public Library (www.sfpl.org).

FIGURE 4.1

Clean storage is critical for preservation.

Courtesy of the Austin History Center, Austin Public Library. Photograph by Grace McEvoy.

Housekeeping is, not surprisingly, also a part of proper handling and preservation of archives and manuscript collections. Most preventative maintenance steps are based on common sense but still bear repeating. Dust user tables regularly without applying chemicals or oils. Furniture polish on tables can transfer to paper materials laid on top of them, including archival folders and rare documents. Some collections contain materials that flake when opened, such as brittle newspaper clippings and brittle bookbindings. Remove any detritus from tables before other materials are placed on the tables, sweep the floors, and empty the trash bins as needed, and on a regular basis. It is also important, even in secure storage areas, to dust shelves on a regular basis, using magnetic wiping cloths that gather dust in rather than simply stirring it up. HEPA (high-efficiency particulate air) vacuums are also recommended because they can be used on and near materials, and only HEPA vacuums will prevent the redistribution of dust back into clean air. Food and drink should not be consumed near collections, nor should food wrappers and bottles be placed in staff trash receptacles. Liquids spilled or dropped on materials can damage them and draw insects, some of which are not visible to the human eye, and those insects will eat just about anything found in the collections. Although food and drinks may be allowed in many parts of the public library, the local history archive will need administrative approvals to restrict its areas. Friendly signs can be posted to alert patrons about restrictions before they enter.

Temperature and humidity control of the stacks, work areas, and reference area is an important part of preservation. An ideal temperature for most people is 70 to 72 degrees Fahrenheit. The ideal temperature for paper, however, is 64 to 68 degrees Fahrenheit with fluctuations of no more than plus or minus five degrees over a 24-hour period. Photographs, computer discs, graphic art, oral history recording tapes, videos, etc., might require lower temperatures. People are comfortable in air at the 40–50 percent relative humidity (RH) level. Optimum humidity for most paper materials is between 30 percent relative humidity and 43 percent relative humidity with fluctuations of no more than plus or minus three degrees within a 24-hour period. Relative humidity for collections is best at a minimum of 30 percent and a maximum of 50 percent. Deterioration progresses at a slower rate when the relative humidity is closer to 30 percent. These conditions are difficult to meet, particularly if the materials are stored in areas where people work, but an attempt should be made to match them as closely as possible and, above all, to keep fluctuations as modest as possible. See the NISO Technical Report TR01–1995, "Environmental Guidelines for the Storage of Paper Records" (National Information Standards Organization, www.niso.org). The report suggests the following environmental parameters for the preservation of

FIGURE 4.2

Work areas and archival storage often need to exist in the same space.

Photograph Courtesy of Melissa Eastin.

paper-based records in libraries and archives: control temperature and relative humidity for combined stack and user areas at 70 degrees maximum, 30–50% RN; for closed stacks 65 degrees maximum, 30–50% RN; and for preservation stacks 30–65 degrees, 30–50% RH.[2]

Cold storage, below 65 degrees (F), with appropriate humidity control can be used in remote storage areas and for on-site areas where little-used materials will be stored. Magnetic media require storage at 40 to 68 degrees (F) with 20 to 45 percent relative humidity. Other formats of materials might also require specialized temperature and humidity controls and special housing. Materials retrieved from cold storage need time to gradually acclimate to room temperature before being used. Significant swings in temperature and humidity create an environment in which molds and insects can flourish and paper and other materials deteriorate. Twenty-four hour monitoring and control of optimal temperature and humidity levels required for the local history archive is expensive and unaffordable for many public library buildings. If library controls automatically turn off air conditioning and heating when the building is closed, a separate climate control unit for the archive is required. If the closed stacks area is the only area that can feasibly receive separate climate control, staff must always return materials to the closed stacks daily. Even if a separate HVAC unit cannot be installed for the department, encourage a regular schedule of replacing all filters in heating and cooling systems to diminish the dust and pollutants in the air, and/or purchase dehumidifiers or humidifiers as needed. Place equipment to monitor and record temperatures and humidity levels throughout storage and work spaces. Some additional helpful steps that aid preservation, security, and disaster preparedness include: locate storage areas away from sprinkler valves and windows; keep materials away from direct sunlight during staff work or users work; use fans to circulate air; if windows are unavoidable, drape them and install glass treated to filter out ultraviolet light; and place ultraviolet light filters on all fluorescent lights in reference areas.

Cooperative agreements, collaboration programs, and consortia arrangements centered on preservation, security, and disaster prevention exist in a number of regions. The Yakima Valley Libraries of central Washington coalesced over several years into an organization that supported the existing libraries with centralized administration, collection management services, and library archives and special collections. "Consequently, local history documents and the many artifacts that had been donated since 1900 to libraries all across central Washington can now be found in the climate-controlled secured storage area for special collections at Yakima Valley Libraries."[3]

Because most archival facilities in the United States are now climate controlled, many potential preservation problems are solved, thus making minimal processing of some collections feasible. The date range and the origin of a collection, plus its inherent value determines the depth of processing and preventative preservation steps that will occur. In minimal processing, for example, documents are not re-foldered unless the original folders are brittle or damaged; fasteners are not removed unless damage is occurring; and clippings, carbons, onionskins, etc. are not segregated nor photocopied; photos are not segregated nor sleeved; encapsulation and mending of torn documents is not completed; nor are scrapbooks and photo albums interleaved. Of course, each collection requires separate evaluation to determine the level of processing required.[4]

Review the local history archive's physical space. Does the area receive direct sunlight that affects the temperature? If the site is in the basement, has flooding occurred in the area? Is the space near any sources of water, such as the kitchen, bathroom, water pipes, or the condenser for the building air conditioning system? Fire prevention is a major concern. Do not locate storage areas near sources of heat and fire, such as a kitchen or heating unit. Fire-resistant walls, floors, and doors should be installed if possible, and smoke detectors should link to the library's security service. Does the department have enough fire extinguishers? What fire suppression system is used? Is it possible to have dry pipe sprinklers with on-off heads that discharge only in the region of a fire and shut off automatically when the fire and smoke are suppressed?[5]

Place emergency supplies within each area where local history archive materials are held or that has been designated as a workspace. Emergency supplies can be purchased from archival storage and supply companies, or the department can create its own. Use a large, wheeled, plastic trash container with a tight cover to hold plastic sheeting, gloves, rubber boots, dust and particle masks, scissors, duct tape, lab coats, paper towels, a utility knife, sponges, a mop, pencils and a notebook, a waterproof document pouch, a disposable cell phone, a flashlight with batteries, two 12-hour light sticks, a small fire extinguisher, a small first aid kit, an emergency instruction sheet, and other appropriate supplies. Such an emergency kit can solve many problems.

If an insect, mold, or mildew problem is found in the stacks and storage areas, before attacking it appraise the affected collections to determine their long-term value. Should these infected collections be deaccessioned? If a collection is to be retained, immediate action must be taken to isolate the affected items away from all other materials. Mold is difficult to control as it can become dormant for periods of time and reactivate in a warm, humid environment. Mold can also migrate and infect previously undamaged materials. Proper treatments include fumigation, freezing, and chemical applications. These can be expensive, and if treatment is done incorrectly might cause more damage. Should the originals be reformatted, thus preserving the information and the infected materials destroyed? A particularly valuable item can be individually conserved.

Although digitized and born-digital materials are increasingly at the center of archival concerns, local history archives and other repositories house thousands of cubic feet of paper collections and continue to accession paper collections. Increasingly, mixed collections containing many different formats—from paper to floppy disks, to records in the cloud, and those harvested from various social media—are accessioned. Despite the increasing variety of formats, many of the reasons for preservation remain the same. Preservation is an ethical responsibility and a core management function. By accepting materials, archivists/librarians are committed to keeping materials and the information they contain safely accessible in their original form for an indefinite period of time. If materials can no longer be kept in original form, then libraries must strive to maintain the information in some other format without compromising the content and context.

Digitization as Access and Preservation

> Analog is a different way of knowing than digital, and each has its intrinsic virtues and limitations. Digital will not and cannot replace analog. To convert everything to digital form would be wrong-headed, even if we could do it. The real challenge is how to make those analog materials more accessible using the powerful tools of digital technology, not only through conversion, but also through digital finding aids and linked databases of search tools.
>
> **—Abby Smith, Why Digitize?**

The basic preservation responsibilities for digital records are the same as those for analog records but also require maintaining equipment to access older technology. The department might be able to upkeep reel-to-reel players, cassette players, and players for vinyl music records, but floppy disk drives and the computers to operate them are hard to acquire and maintain. How many libraries have a first-generation Apple McIntosh, the software to read documents created in WordPerfect 1.0 software, or a computer drive that will read a five-inch floppy disk? A staff person in the local history archive or the library's IT department trained to work with and make accessible digital files created with obsolete technology is required. The Society of American Archivists' Trends in Archives Practice series publications include Digital Preservation Essentials, "Module 12: Preserving Digital Objects," and "Module 13: Digital Preservation Storage." Module 12 focuses on concepts of digital preservation in the archival context, and Module 13 is an introduction to best practices for long-term digital storage. The modules within the series are affordable and available in print, as well as in EPUB and PDF file formats. Further advancements in cataloging digital files and in preserving such files are anticipated each year. Local history archives will benefit by keeping current with "rapidly developing initiatives and best practices" for digital accessibility, preservation, and digital forensics.[6]

A digital program requires planning. Will the project create access or provide preservation, or both? How will the files be used? For access-only programs, create smaller digital images that download quickly from websites and through the Internet. Preservation programs need larger digital images containing more information that can be used in a wide variety of ways and that can be used over a longer period of time. If affordable, it is best to always scan larger preservation files and capture as much information from the original item as possible. This ensures that if the digital file is needed in new ways, not just for the website, materials will not need to be rescanned. Rescanning is often damaging to fragile items.

What will be digitized? Some candidates for digital projects can be identified even before processing begins, such as the papers of an early settler to, and prominent citizen of, Everytown: Rev. Rivers. As processing proceeds, information gathered about the collection will inform decisions, such as will all parts of the collection be digitized or only some parts of the collection? Decisions might be based on the collection's relevance to collecting policies, its condition, historical worth, and user requests. Will digitization become an ongoing program, is it a one-time individual project, or will it become part of a cooperative or consortia program? Each of these programs requires different types of funding and work plans. Funding for individual and cooperative projects can come from grant agencies, but a continuing program needs an ongoing, in-house source of funds. Who is going to do the work? Individual and cooperative projects can be outsourced because the local history archive does not plan nor need to acquire and maintain scanning hardware and software. A vendor will do the work and the quality control, but the department needs to be involved in writing contracts with vendors and checking the work for quality and completeness, and establishing procedures for delivering materials to the vendor or for having the vendor and equipment brought to the library. The parent library's administrative and contracts officers are, of course, required to be involved. An ongoing digital program requires on-site equipment and server storage, staff to do the work, space in which to work, and continued library funding.

Digital management software such as OCLC's CONTENTdm (www.contentdm.org) and Islandora through LYRASIS (www.lyrasisnow.org) can be acquired to manage and present digital images on the Internet. The East Baton Rouge Parish Library's Digital Library is presented through ContentDM. The Amherst Public Library displays its digital images through a Flickr site. There are a number of software options available for presentation of digital assets online. Some are off-the-shelf, ready to implement, and others are open-source applications. CONTENTdm is hosted by a vendor, and Islandora can be hosted by a vendor or by the public library. Omeka is an open-source publishing platform most often used for creating online digital exhibits. Preservation and long-term storage require other applications. Relevant studies and comparisons of available software and implementation concerns are increasingly found in professional literature.

Users increasingly expect digital and online access to the contents of collections, not just to finding aids. Local history archives in public libraries with limited funding might only have a small digital program that can never be its top priority. Balancing priorities and resources is always difficult.[7]

The Baton Rouge Digital Archive

A collection of historical photographs of Baton Rouge and its citizens.

Go to **www.ebrpl.com** and click *Baton Rouge Digital Archive*

We need help identifying photographs!

If you can provide missing information on a particular photograph, please e-mail us at batonrougedigitallibrary@ebrpl.com

FIGURE 4.3

Publicity bookmark about the Baton Rouge Digital Library.

Courtesy of the East Baton Rouge Parish Library.

The Library of Congress suggests that local history archive staff begin to work with donors before acquiring their collections and aid potential donors with the management of their collections. Following the Library of Congress's advice will lead to more accessible collections because they will be easier and cheaper to describe, store, and manage. The Library of Congress's Preservation Division, in conjunction with the National Digital Information Infrastructure and Preservation Program (NDIIPP), advises individuals on how to preserve their digital files. The Library of Congress also encourages libraries to hold Personal Digital Archiving Days, and it provides a kit for planning and organizing the event that can be downloaded from the LOC.gov website. The kit includes the following guides: "Preserving Your Digital Memories," "How Long Will Digital Storage Media Last?" and "Scanning your Personal Collections." The free guides are valuable to researchers and potential donors (visit www.digitalpreservation.gov/personalarchiving/padKit/index.html).

Individuals and families create files of personal information that are valuable to them and to the local history archive. Files that contain community history were formerly paper based, such as letters, financial records, legal documents, photographs, diaries, scrapbooks and newspaper clippings. Digital files contain photographs, digital audio and video files, electronic mail, personal digital records, websites, and social media platform content. The Library of Congress recommendations are not contradictory in regards to archival and library preservation actions, and they were written in a manner to be understood by most people. For example, the Library of Congress recommends that individuals creating and saving digital photographs decide which photos from all storage devices are important to creators and save those of the highest quality—scanned at no less than 300 dpi and preferably 600 dpi. Guidelines also recommend that individuals give the photographs descriptive file names and descriptive subject entries, and create a computer directory/folder structure with a brief description of the directory structure. Keep a printed copy of the photograph inventory with other vital records/ files. Make copies of the photo files and store the copies on at least two (more is better) different media types such as cloud storage, on a computer hard drive, an external hard drive, thumb drives (USBs), CDs or DVDs. Keep the copies physically separate, even in different geographic places, such as one at home and one at work. Check storage copies at least once a year for continued readability and/or corrupt files. Every five years create new digital copies of archival photographs and save them onto new hard drives, new external drives, or cloud storage, for media storage devices have a short life. This procedure is known as refreshing digital files. Remember that the more media are handled and used, the sooner they will become corrupt, and that hardware and software become obsolete. Follow the same Library of Congress recommendations for document, audio, and video files, as well as electronic mail, websites, blogs and social media feeds. The Library of Congress leaflets on Personal Digital Archiving give more specific technical guidance on procedures for scanning personal documents, saving e-mail, naming files, storing files, and systematically refreshing media. Working with users and potential donors to manage and preserve their personal files will help preserve local history. Hopefully, donors can help identify their file contents, the context of the files' creation, and the type of hardware and software used by creators.

Businesses, institutions, organizations, and government agencies have created enormous quantities of electronic records and digital files. Records managers tend to refer to digital records as electronic records but both are created with, and dependent upon, computer hardware and software. The preservation of the data within these files requires a systematic program. Collections received increasingly contain multiple media-storage formats, including CDs, CD-ROMs, multimedia rich e-books, USB drives, and external hard drives, even the computer hard drive and floppy disks. Collections from the late twentieth century might also contain machine-readable records on magnetic tape drives and other storage media from early era computer servers. Any storage media can be damaged and will deteriorate over time; some storage media arrives already scratched and damaged. Since digital files cannot be preserved like a box of papers, how can they be retained? Small local history archives might choose to convert digital files to analog by printing out paper copies because this is the best way to provide access for the department's users. Metadata, such as e-mail headers, from the digital file will not be retainable, but the content and essential context will still exist and be usable when printed. Hyperlinks and searching will no longer be available, but paper keeps well and eliminates the need to maintain obsolete, and current, software and hardware. Large digital files are expensive to print, so only the most requested portions of the collection will be printed for users.[8]

Common digital materials such as personal papers and business documents closely reflect similar paper documents and serve the same function. Electronic systems will track digital materials in ways similar to how paper tracking systems work. Databases have equivalent forms in paper record systems, such as registers, logbooks, journals, payroll records, etc. The OPAC is similar to a paper card catalog, but the OPAC can do complex searching and show interrelationships between information that a card catalog cannot. Digital documents can be linked to many other types of documents to create multimedia content, such as linking digital text to moving images with sound. Digital materials can be stored in a variety of ways (hard drives, thumb drives, CDs) and searched electronically at the word or phrase level, providing a quality of intellectual access almost impossible to deliver in an analog document. Plus, large amounts of digital data can be compressed into relatively small units for more efficient storage.

Metadata contains answers to the questions: who, what, when, where, why, and with whom. Metadata is a generic term that describes information created by the computer, and through metadata the content, context, and structure of documents are described. Unique identifiers for digital objects are also metadata. Metadata exists in non-computer systems as well. For example, finding aids describe the content of a collection and provide context about the creation of historical materials; book indexes provide metadata about the content of books; card catalogs or online catalogs provide metadata about the holdings of a library; and an owner's manual for a lawn mower provides metadata about the machine. Catalog records and finding aids both describe structures of books and collections in terms of their size and their number of pages, boxes, folders, or items, and they both list the presence of images, maps, and other formats. Long-term retention and management of digital materials depends on captured and preserved metadata. Every stage in the life of a digital file has metadata: *technical metadata* describes the equipment used and the time of the file's creation; *use metadata* tracks the access of the file and by whom; *administrative metadata* informs the system and IT staff about how to manage the file; *preservation metadata* documents actions such as migration or emulation; and *discovery metadata* allows a user to find and retrieve information from digital files.

Preservation, security, and access to digital files/electronic records might involve emulation, migration, refreshing, reformatting, and/or normalization.

■ Definitions

Emulation (SAA, 145): This technique seeks to recreate a digital document's original functionality, look, and feel by reproducing, on current computer systems, the behavior of the older system on which the document was created.

Emulation (*ODLIS*): In digital archiving, a preservation technique that employs special software, called an *emulator*, to translate instructions from an original archived software program to enable it to run on a newer platform, obviating the need to preserve obsolete hardware and system software.

Migration (SAA, 252-253): The process of moving data from one information system or storage medium to another to ensure continued access to the information as the system or medium becomes obsolete or degrades over time.

Migration (Dow, 65): To copy data from an old storage medium to a new one.

Refreshing (SAA, 252-253): Copying information onto the same format storage media without any alteration is generally referred to as refreshing.

Reformatting (SAA, 337-338): To create a copy with a format or structure different from the original, especially for preservation or access. Data files may be reformatted so that they can be read by different programs or to counter technological obsolescence.

Reformatting (*ODLIS*): Undertaken when the long-term survival of a document in its current format is unlikely, for example, a work published electronically in a medium rapidly becoming obsolete or a document printed on acid paper in an advanced state of deterioration.

Normalization (Dow, 65): Normalization calls for converting all document types, especially those created by proprietary software, to standard file formats. Normalize digital materials to an open-source format, not depend on any particular software system or hardware, to preserve both documents and the metadata that applies to them.

Corrupt or unreadable files might be accessible through the skills of a computer forensics technician but such work is expensive. Should you keep the digital files if they duplicate the paper files in the collection they came with? Before discarding the files consider access options, but balance the effort required to access and maintain digital files against their importance. Protect computing systems from viruses and other malicious code that might arrive with digital files by reviewing them on a quarantined computer not tied into any network system. Check for malicious code, review the files, and note which file formats are used. Wait 30 days, update the computer's virus detection software, and check the digital files again. Standard archival preservation procedures include using the original media to make a departmental copy and then storing the original. The first copy is used to make several other copies for access. Decide on a standard storage medium and move all electronic records to that medium. As recommended by the Library of Congress, keep multiple copies in multiple locations, including a copy offsite and another uploaded to an online data storage site. If space exists and the IT department approves, install a copy in the local history archive network for future access. Keep the original electronic records in their original media and formats, and be sure the originals, the first copies, and the access copies all bear the same labels and metadata. The metadata required by each department will vary depending on needs and future plans. Create metadata about the structure and layout of the files, and information about files and relationships with other files in the collection (for example, title, originator, classification and indexing, and distribution).[9]

Accept that there is no way to ensure the long-term preservation of digital files created in obsolete hardware and software, but still develop a preservation plan for them. Most computer storage media can be counted on to last for about five years—some types last longer under ideal conditions. How will users access the contents? Digital files can be provided through the library's intranet and websites, through a patron workstation, by providing copies of digital files to patrons on request, or a combination of these. Electronic files should be organized as part of the collection regardless of the access method and the description of digital files should be equal to the levels of description and standards used for paper records and all collections.[10]

Review the OCLC Research publication "Walk This Way: Detailed Steps for Transferring Born-Digital Content from Media You Can Read In-house" (www.oclc.org/content/dam/research/publications/library/2013/2013–02 .pdf). This report was designed for archives that begin as born-digital projects, especially projects containing born-digital collections received from donors. It is a procedural guide to transferring digital materials received on a wide variety of storage devices and it explains how to document what is done. Staff with various skills can follow and successfully use these guidelines. See also "Getting Started with Digitization: An Introduction for Libraries," a TechSoup webinar available at https://www.webjunction.org.

Websites contain and make accessible important local history information. If a website's content were on paper would you keep it? If yes, then you must consider keeping the web pages. Web pages are presented in HTML, an open-source format used worldwide, therefore a server can easily be used to host and preserve web pages, or they can be stored on a web archiving service such as the Internet Archive. For the past 20 years, The Internet Archive (https://www.archive.org) has built a digital library of Internet sites and other cultural artifacts in digital form and saved the history of billions of web pages. Its purpose is to preserve and create access for anyone who wishes to use the information.

In less than two decades, the digital information revolution has created unprecedented access, but it has also fueled an unprecedented demand for access. The local history archive might increasingly focus on providing better access to analog collections through the development of digitization programs, as well as ensure that born-digital records and other electronic materials are collected and made accessible. Digitized materials are user-friendly surrogates for original materials. Digital projects can support the public library user's need to have access to archives and manuscripts remotely and at all hours.

Preservation Checklist

Checklists illustrate that many of the same steps, actions, and requirements appear under the responsibilities of preservation, security, and disaster preparedness and recovery.

A staff member is assigned primary responsibility for preservation (all staff must assume some preservation activities).

- Name of primary [*insert name*]
- Backup person [*insert name*]

1. The local history archive has proper temperature and humidity with minimal fluctuations and consistent monitoring at all times, even when other parts of the library are not controlled.
2. The local history archive has an area in which to segregate insect- and mold-infested materials, and it has designated eradication procedures.
3. User rules are posted on the local history archive website and a printed copy is given to each new user. User rules require, among others, that hands are washed prior to handling materials; users should not use hand sanitizers and hand lotions while handling materials; all items should be handled carefully and kept in their original order; items must remain on the table during use and not placed in the user's lap or propped on other items; gloves must be worn to handle certain items; and cameras that do not use flash can be used but only for specific materials.
4. Boxes are labeled, even with temporary labels, to speed arrangement and description, secure materials, and prevent the disaster of lost materials.
5. Food and liquids are allowed only in specified areas. Food and liquids are not allowed in the local history archive.

6. Furniture and shelving is dusted and cleaned without using furniture polish or other chemicals and floors are regularly cleaned. The removal of dirt and dust from collections and from storage spaces is routine. A HEPA filter vacuum cleaner and magnetic wiping cloths are used.

7. Storage areas are located away from sprinkler valves, windows, sunlight, rain, and wind; materials are kept away from direct sunlight during staff work or users work; fans are used to circulate air when needed; windows are draped or contain glass treated to filter out ultraviolet light; and ultraviolet light filters are on all fluorescent lights in work and reference areas.

8. Donors supply a listing of materials to be appraised for possible acquisition.

9. Rate the environment in which potential collections were housed before being accessioned: Very good Good Fair Poor Very poor

10. During processing, items needing individual and specialized conservation, reformatting, and/or candidates for digitization are identified.

11. Digital projects are planned with the preservation needs of digital files identified and a program established for handling them when first received and for long-term preservation and for making them accessible.

12. Electronic/digital files on all types of media are reviewed on a stand-alone computer, not connected to any library network or the Internet, to prevent malware within the files from entering the library's computer systems.

Notes regarding actions needed:

Add other checklist questions as needed for the specific local history archive.

■ Preservation Needs Assessment Worksheet Example —————

1. Describe the needed preservation actions identified during appraisal/accessioning.
   - Collection number:
   - Collection name:
2. List all items in the collection for which preservation needs were identified. Basic procedures such as dusting and re-boxing can be listed or only needs for items in less than good condition.

Type of Material	Quantity	Condition and Needed Actions	Completed on, by
Civil War letters	50 items	Tears to repair, stains to remove	8/20/17 FP

Type of Material	Quantity	Condition and Needed Actions	Completed on, by
Photographs	CD-ROM 3 CDs	Was stored in humid, hot attic, transfer if possible to computer	11/4/17 FP
Rolled maps	22 items	Humidify and flatten	12/9/17 FP
Handwritten 1806 diary	1 vol.	Pages loose, some writing smeared, torn and brittle paper—outsource to conservator	1/4/18 FP

3. Establish a database for tracking items outsourced to a qualified conservator. Request a quote for work before authorizing the conservator to proceed. File correspondence and other documents related to repairs in the collection's accession file.

SECURITY

Security is an important part of preservation. If something goes missing you aren't preserving it. Security issues and concerns appear throughout the reference services and user access procedures. Security awareness begins at the first encounter with each collection as the potential acquisition is reviewed and appraised for possible accessioning. Where are the materials to be physically reviewed and appraised? If in the donor's office, for example, does the donor have an inventory or basic list of what the local history archive staff should be reviewing? As the appraisal proceeds, share the listing of materials created with the donor, but do not share the staff's appraisal notes about the collection. An informed donor will make Processing Step 2: Legal Transfer, and the deed of gift process go more smoothly.

The local history archive can best serve users, and security, by having a central, continually staffed reference desk where users ask questions and receive assistance. Staff members must never leave the reading room or user research area unattended. Arrange tables and all work areas in the reading room so that they are clearly visible by a staff member at all times. Staffs who learn to monitor the activities in the reading area systematically, and who accept the responsibility for enforcing rules, improve security. It is very important to know the location of closed stack materials at all times.

FIGURE 4.4

User tables are visible to staff through the office glass window.

Photograph Courtesy of Melissa Eastin.

Require users to present a valid photo ID even if registration is not required. Registration and requests for materials can be done through computer systems rather than in paper forms. User registration serves three purposes: statistical, informational, and as a deterrent to theft.

Other reading room and reference rules apply to safe handling as well as security. Designated user tables for research, or a separate local history archive reference room, along with staff-only storage and shelving areas, are necessary. The items and personal tools users can have with them might include pencils, loose paper, tablets, and laptop computers without cases. Computer cases, bags, purses, notebooks, binders, ink pens, indelible markers, and food and drink are not allowed. Why? What harm, for example, can be done with a purse or bag? An item from a collection can be inadvertently brushed off the table into a bag and removed from the library. Such action is not always inadvertent —thieves do visit public libraries.

Appropriate tracking procedures for retrieval of materials for users and re-shelving are important security measures as well. Requests from users for access to materials should be through an archival management software program or through paper based systems. When items are retrieved for a user, a method of call slips identifies what is being removed by name of collection and box number as well as the location to where the material should be returned. A copy of the call slip stays on the shelf and another copy goes with the items removed from the shelf and delivered to the reference area. Also, it is critical to show which staff member removed the material and which staff member re-shelved it. First, this proves units of a collection have been removed from the shelf for a legitimate reason. Second, statistics are derived from the call slip, such as when was it retrieved, who is the user, which part of the collection (box, folder, reel, computer disk, etc.) is being used, who pulled the material, when was it re-shelved and by whom. If mis-shelved, a documented trail of actions related to the missing material is available.

In addition to the physical arrangement and monitoring of the space where patrons use materials, other aspects of the local history archive space must be reviewed. Many of these aspects overlap with preservation and disaster prevention steps. Is there a closed stack area for storage or a designated shelving arrangement where patrons are not allowed to enter? Are materials reshelved each day in secure areas? Are the door locks keyed separately from door locks in other areas of the public library? Is a log kept listing the staff members with keys to these door locks, such as those with access to administrative offices, the facilities manager, the overall library security officer, and others? The number of master keys that unlock all doors should be limited and master keys should not be copied without the security officer/administrator's approval. Each day at closing, master keys and all keys to storage areas should be secured. Local history archive staff must never remove master keys from the building and should carry only necessary entry keys home. Are separate security alarms placed in the local history archive? Do cameras monitor the area? Are doors alarmed? Is a loading dock nearby for ease in transferring archival materials, and is the storage area near the freight elevator with keyed access to the storage area from the elevator? Is the floor strong enough to hold the weight of archival materials? Is the space secure enough for archival materials? Can all the exits be locked and/or can fire exits have doors with breakaway bars and alarms installed?

Security Checklist

Staff member with primary responsibility for security (all staff must assume some security activities):

- Name of primary [*insert name*]
- Backup person [*insert name*]

Checklists illustrate that the steps, actions, and requirements under the responsibilities of preservation, security, and disaster preparedness and recovery overlap and that each one builds on the others. After completing the *Preservation Checklist,* complete the *Security Checklist.*

1. Users are required to register and wear ID badges.
2. Staff members are required to wear ID badges.
3. Staff is trained to properly observe users and the materials being used.
4. Designated tables or a separate local history archive reference room exist.
5. Staff-only storage and shelving areas are available.
6. Computer cases, bags, purses, notebooks, binders, ink pens, indelible markers, and food and drink are not allowed.
7. Establish and maintain a tracking system for materials that indicates what, when, and by whom materials are removed from storage and returned to storage.
8. Physical space concerns: review all areas, including reference, stacks, workspace, etc. Address any security concerns: Is a loading dock nearby for ease in transferring archival materials and is the storage area in close proximity to the freight elevator with keyed access to the storage from the elevator? Is the floor strong enough to hold the weight of archival materials? Is the space secure enough for archival materials?
9. Managing locks and keys: The local history archive's door locks are keyed separately from door locks in other areas of the public library. All exits can be locked and/or exits needed as fire exits have doors with breakaway bars and alarms installed. A log is kept listing the staff members with door keys. The master keys that unlock all local history archive doors are limited and master keys are not copied. Each day at closing, master keys and all keys to storage areas are secured. Areas have separate security alarms and cameras are monitored.

Notes regarding actions needed:

Add other checklist questions as needed for the specific local history archive.

DISASTER AWARENESS, PREVENTION, AND RECOVERY

Who is responsible for disaster awareness and assessment, and prevention planning and recovery response at the library? The local history archive will be only one department represented in the planning and recovery processes. Overall responsibility lies with the library administration and it delegates actions to appropriate staff to carry out. Larger libraries might have a security officer and/or security office, and the disaster team might or might not reside in that department, with or without a disaster prevention officer. In a very small public library with an equally small local history archive, the department head might be the official or de-facto disaster officer as well as the security officer, by virtue of the rare and unique materials contained in the local history archive. The department must adequately represent itself as an active member of the disaster prevention and recovery planning and implementation team in the public library.

Disasters primarily include fire, water, wind, and earthquake damage. Disasters can be caused by nature and by people. Disaster preparedness includes assessing threats, eliminating threats, initiating proactive preventative measures, developing a plan, and talking about the issues. Carry out an assessment of possible threats that includes an identification of fire hazards such as electrical wiring with signs of aging and fraying in all storage and work areas. What are the natural disasters that have occurred, and that might occur again, in the geographical location of the library? Eliminate the threats that are found or might occur. Initiate proactive preventative measures. Are fire alarm and switch boxes always locked? In the event of heat failure, does the local history archive have a low temperature alarm, to prevent frozen pipes? Are fire drills and disaster drills performed on a regular basis? The final element of preservation is disaster planning and recovery. Do not be complacent.

■ Example Disaster Plans

In 2009, The State Library of Ohio (www.library.ohio.gov) developed a "Disaster Preparedness Plan for Small Public Libraries", which is, despite its title, applicable to any size public library. It is a step-by-step guide to follow while developing a disaster preparedness plan. Compare your public library's plan to its guidelines. The plan can be found on the ERIC website (www.eric.ed.gov) by search using its Eric Number, ED481308, or using the plan's title. Other helpful resources are also available at WebJunction (www.webjunction.org/), such as: TechSoup's "Disaster Planning and Recovery Toolkit," a guide to rebuilding the library's technological infrastructure after a disaster.

For an example of a local disaster plan, see the Huntsville-Madison County (Alabama) Public Library Disaster Plan (www.hmcpl.org, linked from the "Using the Library, About HMCPL" tabs). The introduction states:

> Because all libraries are susceptible to disasters, The Huntsville-Madison County Public Library is committed to maintaining a vigilant state of disaster preparedness for staff, the collection and our facilities. Enlightened self-interest tells us that to be prepared is the greatest weapon against disaster. This plan, along with continual training, provides library staff with a set of disaster priorities, emergency procedure guidelines and floor plans for each location.

Another example is the Livonia Public Library, Livonia, New York "2012 Disaster Plan, Prevention/Preparation" (www.livonialibrary.org, under the Library Policy and Plans tab, Disaster Plan link). The introduction states:

> This plan will aid in the successful resolution and recovery in dealing with the aftermath of a disaster, whether it be fire, water/wind damage, vandalism, bomb threat, or bug infestation, with no loss of life if the occurrence takes place during library hours. In addition, it is hoped that prior planning and quick implementation of this plan will limit damage to the collection, equipment, and the building.

For libraries and local history archives, it is imperative to have a written disaster plan with procedures that designate someone to coordinate and carry out disaster-related activities. Within a public library, departments will need to work together, but certain aspects of the plan can be carried out in the microsystem of the local history archive. For example, after a disaster, check the space for further damage, document any damage, gather supplies for the area, move damaged materials to a designated space, and identify what steps— coordinated to specific damages—are to be taken. The recovery procedures for the library and the local history archive must clearly detail what is to be done, by whom, where, and when. The disaster prevention and recovery plan details a current list of staff responsibilities, contact information, and call trees with phone numbers and e-mail addresses, all updated consistently. Remember that in many disasters cell phone towers will stop functioning for indeterminate times. Gather staff's non-work e-mail addresses and landline telephone numbers, as well as family contact information. If your staff is forced to evacuate the community, town, or even the state, where will they go? These actions are everyone's responsibility, especially knowing who their department leader is and who they are responsible for contacting, working with, replacing, etc. Talk about the issues. What is considered a disaster and what are the fears, concerns, and positive approaches? Ask each person to assess possible threats in their workroom, cubicle, office, etc., and present possible reactions needed. What can be fixed now, such as frayed wiring or overloaded plug-in strips, so it does not create a future disaster? Ask staff to list the materials that should be saved first from the local history archive. It should not be necessary to remind everyone that the lives of people come before even the most valuable and precious item. It is the duty of all to read and understand the disaster prevention and recovery plan.

Disaster Prevention, Preparedness, and Recovery Checklist

Staff member with primary responsibility for disaster preparedness (all staff must assume some disaster preparedness): Name of primary [insert name] Backup person [insert name]

Checklists illustrate that the steps, actions, and requirements that are under the responsibilities of preservation, security, and disaster preparedness and recovery overlap and that each one builds upon the others. After completing the *Preservation Checklist* and the *Security Checklist*, complete the *Disaster Prevention, Preparedness, and Recovery Checklist*:

1. Write a disaster prevention, preparedness, and recovery plan for the local history archive specifically as a component of the parent library's plan. Establish a program to familiarize all staff members with the plan and their responsibilities as specified within components of the plan.

2. Label boxes, even using temporary labels, as appropriate through all processing steps, to begin the process of securing materials and to prevent the disaster of lost materials.

3. Carry out an assessment of possible threats. Which natural disasters have occurred, and might occur again, in the geographical location of the library? Identify fire, water, and temperature hazards in all areas. Eliminate the threats that are found, or that might occur, by initiating proactive preventative measures. Are fire drills and disaster drills performed on a regular basis?

4. Physical space review: Are fire and alarm switch boxes always locked? Does the local history archive have a low temperature alarm in the event of heat failure to prevent frozen pipes? Does the area receive direct sunlight that affects the temperature of the area? If the archive site is in the basement, has flooding occurred in the area? Is the area near any sources of water, such as the kitchen, bathroom, water pipes, or the condenser for the building air conditioner? Do not locate storage areas near sources of heat and fire such as a kitchen or heating unit. Fire-resistant walls, floors, and doors should be installed if possible and smoke detectors should link to the library's security service. Does the local history archive have enough fire extinguishers? What fire suppression system is used? Is it possible to have dry pipe sprinklers with on-off heads that discharge only in the region of a fire and shut off automatically when the fire and smoke are suppressed?

5. The disaster prevention and recovery plan must include a current list of staff, including their contact information and the assigned disaster responsibilities of all staff. Update consistently. Telephone call trees and e-mail contact lists are required.

Notes regarding actions needed:

Add other checklist questions as needed for the specific local history archive.

For the proper care of the local history archive, the functions and responsibilities of preservation, security, disaster awareness and prevention planning must overlap everywhere and always. As the caretakers of our local history, we collect and *preserve* to make materials accessible.

NOTES

1. Gregory S. Hunter, *Preserving Digital Information: A How-To-Do-It Manual* (New York: Neal Schuman Publishers, 2000), 3.
2. Carmicheal, *Organizing Archival Records*, 74.
3. Walker, "Local Treasures," 19–20.
4. Hackbart-Dean and Slomba, *How to Manage Processing*, 30–36; Janet Hauck, "How to Get More 'Product' While Doing Less 'Process'," *Archival Outlook*, May/June 2008.
5. Chad Leinaweaver, "Band-Aids and Superglue for the Cash-Strapped Local History Preservation Librarian," in Smallwood, *Preserving Local Writers*, 5; Yakel, *Starting an Archives*, 58–59; 61–66.
6. Bastian, Sniffin-Marinoff and Webber, *Archives in Libraries*, 69–70; Digital Public Library of America http://bit.ly/dplaCollections; Abby Smith, *Why Digitize?* Council on Library and Information Resources, 80 (1999), 15.
7. Christine Wiseman and Al Matthews, "Time, Money, and Effort: A Practical Approach to Digital Content Management" (2016). *AUC Robert W. Woodruff Library Staff Publications*. Paper 8, http://digitalcommons.auctr.edu/libpubs/8; Jill Marie Koelling, *Digital Imaging: A Practical Approach* (Walnut Creek, CA: AltaMira Press, 2004), 11–14; Hunter, *Preserving Digital Information*, 113, 132.
8. Elizabeth H. Dow, *Electronic Records in the Manuscript Repository* (Lanham, MD: Scarecrow Press, 2009), 25–26, 33–24, 63–69.
9. Dearstyne, *Managing Historical Records Programs*, 150.
10. Hackbart-Dean and Slomba, *How to Manage Processing*, 48–52; Carmicheal, *Organizing Archival Records*, 72–73; Dow, *Electronic Records*, 74–75, 92, 112.

CONCLUSION

IN EACH CHAPTER of this book, examples from public libraries with local history archives are given. These examples can be used in many ways as you plan, develop, and implement programs for your local history archive. Contacting library staff at the example libraries can also be helpful for answering questions and expanding your professional network. A network of colleagues helps in many ways, including as a sounding board for new ideas or refinement of old ones, giving advice on avoiding mistakes, and as teachers for local history archive staff members. Please remember that web addresses and links change; thus, if a website address does not open in your browser, search using the name of the organization or publication title.

On a daily basis, self-directed continuing education is a commitment to professional improvement, and it demonstrates a willingness to empower departments by broadening staff knowledge. Many resources are cost free but, of course, require time. Everyone benefits from being encouraged to be part of a professionally active team. Staffs receive continuing education and bring increased knowledge to the job from active involvement in appropriate organizations. Many professional membership groups provide workshops on the basics of archives, collections handling and care, and other relevant topics, and they publish valuable books, journals, technical guidelines, and standards. Continuing education for caretakers of local history archives is needed with discussion centering on the best use of theoretical publications as well as attending classes and seeking assistance from colleagues. Pay for these positions has been and probably always will be low for professional workers, so educational funds must be maximized. Join one professional association at the national level and at a minimum one state or regional organization.

The two most relevant national professional membership organizations are the Society of American Archivists (www.archivists.org) and the American Library Association (www.ala.org). Both provide many continuing education workshops on topics important to local history archives. These offerings change topics and are updated often. The Society of American Archivists is organized by sections and roundtables—for example, the Public Library Archives/Special Collections Roundtable (PLASC). The American Library Association is organized by divisions, such as: the Reference and User Services Association (RUSA), the History Section, the Local History Committee, the Association of College and Research Libraries (ACRL), and the Rare Books and Manuscripts Section (RBMS), which have various discussion groups and committees. SAA has free publications, such as *Describing Archives: A Content Standard*, 2nd edition, updated in 2015. ALA Online Learning provides free webinars. The Academy of Certified Archivists (www.certifiedarchivists .org) presents its Exam Handbook online under the tab "Becoming a Certified Archivist." Reviewing the Exam Handbook is an excellent learning experience even if you do not plan to take the exam.

Membership in the SAA and the ALA, even though it is based on the income of the member or offered at special rates for various categories of members, is expensive, but state and regional professional membership organizations fulfill continuing education needs for lower fees. Travel to regional or state workshops and meetings can also be much cheaper. Regional archival organizations include those such as the Society of Southwest Archivists (www .southwestarchivists.org) and the Mid-Atlantic Regional Archives Conference (www.marac.info/). State organizations include those such as the Society of Georgia Archivists (www.soga.org) and the Society of California Archivists (www.calarchivists.org). State library associations include those such as the Texas Library Association (www.txla.org) and the Louisiana Library Association (https://lla.online.org/). Some cities have archival organizations, such as the Chicago Area Archivists (www.chicagoarchivists.org).

There are regional groups to help as well. For example, see WESTPAS (Western States and Territories Preservation Assistance Service) at www .westpas.org. WESTPAS delivers preservation education and training workshops to libraries, archives, museums, historical societies, and other cultural institutions in 14 participating states and territories. Workshops are free to attend and the workshop documents are extremely helpful and available for free download. Other regional and state consortiums, such as LYRASIS (www .lyrasisnow.org) and Amigos Library Services (www.amigos.org) also provide workshops on a variety of important topics including preservation, disaster prevention, and digital libraries. Their workshops and courses are offered online as well as in on-site classes.

LYRASIS offers many online courses throughout each year. For example, a four-hour online class that is designed to help archivists and librarians identify common photographic processes and develop sensible and economical preservation strategies for these materials. In addition to learning to identify various types of photographs, attendees learn about preservation issues with prints, color, film, glass, and photograph albums. Students also learn about the proper environment and storage for their collections and discuss handling, housing, and security. The costs of online courses vary depending on personal or library memberships in the sponsoring organization such as LYRASIS, SAA, ALA, etc. Archival recertification credits are also offered for many of the classes and workshops. Those who are Certified Archivists through the Society of American Archivists' Certification Program will want to accumulate recertification credits.

Amigos Library Services (https://www.amigos.org/) offers online conferences and many continuing education classes, some with reduced registration costs. Some course titles are: "Digital Preservation @ Your Library: You Can Do This!," "Introduction to the Encoded Archival Description," and "Social Media Close-Up." Basic and refresher classes on reference topics are also offered.

Websites such as "WebJunction: The learning place for libraries," (https://www.webjunction.org) makes some of its webinars available online free of charge. Also at the WebJunction site are self-paced courses from management to marketing and others such as "Building a Positive Social Media Presence," and TechSoup's "Disaster Planning and Recovery Toolkit," a guide to rebuilding the library's technological infrastructure after a disaster. Utilize these helpful sources.

I began *Creating a Local History Archive at Your Public Library* with the hope and wish that administrators, leaders, and staffs will find the book a manual of practice, and a guide to extensive information on providing access to, and caretaking of, local history collections. I end with the same hope and look forward to continued networking with the public library local history archive community in the future.

BIBLIOGRAPHY

BOOKS AND BOOK CHAPTERS

American Library Association. "Guidelines for the Formulation of Collection Development Policies," in Wallach John Bonk and Rose Mary Magrill, eds. *Building Library Collections*, 5th ed. Metuchen, NJ: Scarecrow Press, 1979, 363–368.

Bastian, Jeannette A., Megan Sniffin-Marinoff and Donna Webber. *Archives in Libraries: What Librarians and Archivists Need to Know to Work Together.* Chicago: Society of American Archivists, 2015.

Behrnd-Klodt, Menzi, and Christopher J. Prom, eds. *Rights in the Digital Era.* Chicago: Society of American Archivists, 2015.

Carmicheal, David W. *Organizing Archival Records: A Practical Method of Arrangement and Description for Small Archives.* 3rd ed. Walnut Creek, CA: AltaMira Press, 2012.

Cooke, Robert A. "Managing Change in Organizations," in Gerald Zaltman, ed. *Management Principles for Nonprofit Agencies and Organizations.* New York: American Management Association, 1979.

Cox, Richard J. *Managing Institutional Archives: Foundational Principles and Practices.* Westport, CT: Greenwood Press, 1992.

Cox, Richard J. *Managing Records as Evidence and Information.* Westport, CT: Quorum Books, 2001.

Dearstyne, Bruce W. *Managing Historical Records Programs: A Guide for Historical Agencies.* Walnut Creek, CA: AltaMira Press, 2000.

Dow, Elizabeth H. *Creating EAD-Compatible Finding Guides on Paper.* Lanham, MD: Scarecrow Press, 2005.

Dow, Elizabeth H. *Electronic Records in the Manuscript Repository.* Lanham, MD: Scarecrow Press, 2009.

Griffin, Emily. "Tracing History through Nontraditional Methods," in Smallwood and Williams, *Preserving Local Writers*, 316–324.

Hackbart-Dean, Pam, and Elizabeth Slomba. *How to Manage Processing in Archives and Special Collections*. Chicago: Society of American Archivists, 2012.

Helling, William. "Creating Local History Collection Development Guidelines," in Smallwood and Williams, *Preserving Local Writers*, 105–115.

Hirsch, Robert. *Seizing the Light: A History of Photography*. Boston: McGraw-Hill, 2000.

Hunter, Gregory S. *Developing and Maintaining Practical Archives: A How-To-Do-It Manual*. 3rd ed. New York: Neal Schuman Publishers, 2017.

Hunter, Gregory S. *Preserving Digital Information: A How-To-Do-It Manual*. New York: Neal Schuman Publishers, 2000.

James, Russell D. and Peter J. Wosh, eds. *Public Relations and Marketing for Archives: A How-To-Do-It Manual*. Chicago: Society of American Archivists, 2011.

Kammen, Carol. *On Doing Local History*. 2nd ed. Walnut Creek, CA: AltaMira Press, 2003.

Kammen, Carol and Norma Prendergast, eds. *Encyclopedia of Local History*. 2nd ed. Lanham, MD: AltaMira Press, 2013.

Koelling, Jill Marie. *Digital Imaging: A Practical Approach*. Walnut Creek, CA: AltaMira Press, 2004.

Lehman, Katharine, ed. *Interacting with History: Teaching with Primary Sources*. Chicago: ALA Editions, 2014.

Leinaweaver, Chad. "Band-Aids and Superglue for the Cash-Strapped Local History Preservation Librarian," in Smallwood, *Preserving Local Writers*, 3–10.

Levien, Roger E. "Confronting the Future: Strategic Visions for the 21st Century Public Library" ALA Office for Information Technology Policy, *Policy Brief 4* (June 2011).

Marquis, Kathy and Leslie Waggener. *Local History Reference Collections for Public Libraries*. Chicago: ALA Editions, 2015.

Meringola, Denise D. *Museums, Monuments, and National Parks*. Amherst: University of Massachusetts Press, 2012.

Moran, Barbara B., Robert D. Stueart and Claudia Morner. *Library and Information Center Management*. 8th ed. Santa Barbara, CA: Libraries Unlimited, 2013.

Pearce-Moses, Richard. *A Glossary of Archival and Records Terminology*. Chicago: Society of American Archivists. www.2archivists.org/glossary.

Phillips, Faye. *Local History Collections in Libraries*. Englewood, CO: Libraries Unlimited, 1995.

Reitz, Joan M. *Online Dictionary for Library and Information Science*. Santa Barbara, CA: ABC-CLIO, 2004–2014. www.abc-clio.com/ODLIS/odlis_A.aspx.

Ritzenthaler, Mary Lynn, Diane Vogt-O'Connor, Helena Zinkham, Brett Carnell, and Kit Peterson. *Photographs: Archival Care and Management*. Chicago: Society of American Archivists, 2006.

Smallwood, Carol and Elaine Williams, eds. *Preserving Local Writers, Genealogy, Photographs, Newspapers, and Related Materials*. Lanham, MD: Scarecrow Press, 2012.

Smith, Abby. *Why Digitize?* The Council on Library and Information Resources, 80, 1999.

Smith, Page. *As a City Upon a Hill: The Town in American History.* New York: Alfred A. Knopf, 1966.

Society of American Archivists. *Describing Archives: A Content Standard (DACS).* Chicago: SAA, 2013, updated 2015. For a complete list of and links to archival standards, see http://www2.archivists.org/standards.

Society of American Archivists. *Guidelines for Reappraisal and Deaccessioning.* Chicago: SAA, 2007. For a complete list of and links to archival standards, see http://www2.archivists.org/standards.

Thompson, Enid, *Local History Collections: A Manual for Librarians.* Nashville, TN: American Association for State and Local History, 1978.

Trachtenberg, Alan. *Reading American Photographs: Images as History, Mathew Brady to Walker Evans.* New York: Hill and Wang, 1989.

United States. Office of Education. *Public libraries in the US of America; their history, condition, and management. Special report, Department of the Interior, Bureau of Education. Part I.* Washington, DC: Government Printing Office, 1876.

Welland, Susan. "Managing Archives in Local History Collections," in Smallwood and Williams, *Preserving Local Writers,* 146–156.

Wiegand, Wayne A. *Part of Our Lives: A People's History of the American Public Library.* New York: Oxford University Press, 2015.

Yakel, Elizabeth. *Starting an Archives.* Chicago: Society of American Archivists, 1994.

ARTICLES

Beasley, Carla. "Forsyth County Public Library Strategic Planning, 2013–2018." *Georgia Library Quarterly,* 50 (Article 1, 2013): 19–27. http://digitalcommons.kennesaw.edu/glq/v0150/iss2/1.

Casey, Anne Marie. "Strategic Priorities: A Roadmap through Change for Library Leaders." *Library Leadership & Management* 29 (February 2015): 1–16.

Cox, Robert S. "Maximal Processing, or, Archivist on a Pale Horse." *Journal of Archival Organization* 8 (2010): 134–148.

Digital Public Library of America, Archival Description Working Group, "Aggregating and Representing Collections in the Digital Public Library of America." 2016. http://bit.ly/dplaCollections.

Glazer, Gwen. "Digitizing Hidden Collections in Public Libraries." *OITP Perspectives* 1 (June 2011): 1–9.

Greene, Mark and Dennis Meissner, "More Product, Less Process: Revamping Traditional Archival Processing." *American Archivist* 68 (Fall/Winter 2005): 208–263.

"Gwinnett County Public Library, GCPL Announces Strategic Plan." *Georgia Library Quarterly* 52, Article 15 (2015): 1–2. www.gwinnettpl.org and http://digital commons.kennesaw.edu/cgi/viewcontent.cgi?article=1899&context=glq.

Hauck, Janet. "How to Get More 'Product' While Doing Less 'Process'." *Archival Outlook* (May/June 2008): 6–7.

Koizumi, Masanori. "Transitions in Public Library Management: From the International Perspective of Strategy, Organizational Structure, and Operations." *Journal of Library Administration* 54 (November 2014): 659–690.

Linderman, Eric. "Archives in Public Libraries." *Public Libraries* 48 (January/ February 2009): 46–51.

Ness, David L. book review, *Indiana Magazine of History* 75 (1996): 369–371.

Phillips, Faye. "Developing Collecting Policies for Manuscript Collections." *American Archivist* 47 (Winter 1984): 3042.

Walker, Terry. "Local Treasures: The Value of Special Collections in the Public Library Setting." Washington Library Association, *Alki* (July 2014): 18–23.

Whittaker, Beth M., "'Get It, Catalog It, Promote It': New Challenges to Providing Access to Special Collections." *RBM: A Journal of Rare Books, Manuscripts and Cultural Heritage* 7 (Fall 2006): 121–133.

Williams, Jeff, Tammy Nickelson Dearie, Brian E. C. Schottlaender. "Bottom-Up Strategic Planning: The UC San Diego Libraries Experience." *Library Leadership & Management* 27 (2013): 1–12.

Wiseman, Christine and Al Matthews, "Time, Money, and Effort: A Practical Approach to Digital Content Management." *AUC Robert W. Woodruff Library Staff Publications.* 2016, Paper 8. http://digitalcommons.auctr.edu/libpubs/8.

INDEX